Ninth Workshop on Speech and Language Processing for Assistive Technologies (SLPAT 2022)

Dublin, Ireland
27 May 2022

ISBN: 978-1-7138-6751-7

Printed from e-media with permission by:

Curran Associates, Inc.
57 Morehouse Lane
Red Hook, NY 12571

Some format issues inherent in the e-media version may also appear in this print version.

Printed with permission by Curran Associates, Inc. (2023)

Association for Computational Linguistics
209 N. Eighth Street
Stroudsburg, Pennsylvania 18360

Phone: 1-570-476-8006
Fax: 1-570-476-0860

acl@aclweb.org

Additional copies of this publication are available from:

Curran Associates, Inc.
57 Morehouse Lane
Red Hook, NY 12571 USA
Phone: 845-758-0400
Fax: 845-758-2633
Email: curran@proceedings.com
Web: www.proceedings.com

SLPAT 2022

The Ninth Workshop on Speech and Language Processing for Assistive Technologies

Proceedings of the Workshop

May 27, 2022

Introduction

We are pleased to bring you the Proceedings of the Ninth Workshop on Speech and Language Processing for Assistive Technologies (SLPAT-2022), held in virtually and in Dublin, Ireland on May 27, 2022. This workshop was intended to bring researchers from all areas of speech and language technology with a common interest in making everyday life more accessible for people facing physical, cognitive, sensory, emotional or developmental communication challenges. This workshop builds on eight previous such workshops co-located with conferences such as ACL, NAACL, EMNLP and Interspeech. It provides an opportunity for researchers, clinicians, and users of assistive technology to share research findings, to discuss present and future challenges, and to explore the potential for collaboration and progress. While Augmentative and Alternative Communication (AAC) is a particularly apt application area for speech and natural language processing technologies, we purposefully made the scope of the workshop broad enough to include assistive technologies (AT) as a whole, even those falling outside of AAC. Thus we have aimed at broad inclusivity, which is also manifest in the diversity of our program committee, authors, and invited speakers. We thank all the people who made this event possible.

Sarah Ebling, Emily Prud'hommeaux, and Preethi Vaidyanathan
Co-organizers of SLPAT-2022

Program Committee

Workshop Organizers

Sarah Ebling, University of Zurich
Emily Prud'hommeaux, Boston College
Preethi Vaidyanathan, EyeGaze, Inc.

Program Committee

Sara Candeias, Microsoft
Cecilia Ovesdotter Alm, Rochester Institute of Technology
Didier Schwab, Université Grenoble Alpes
Kay Chen Chen, University of New Hampshire, Durham
Roelant Ossewaarde, University of Groningen
Andre Coy, University Of the West Indies Mona
Andrew Fowler, Nuance Communications
Brian Roark, Google
Catherine Middag, Interuniversitair Micro-Electronica Centrum
Corinne Fredouille, Avignon University
Daniel Korzekwa, Amazon
Dean Neumann, Visionary Research Inc.
Enno Hermann, Idiap Research Institute
François Portet, Université Grenoble Alpes
Fraser Shein, Quillsoft Ltd.
Gayatri Venugopal, Symbiosis International, Deemed University
Gloria Gagliardi, University of Bologna
Jan Oliver Wülfing, University of Augsburg, Universität Augsburg
Kathleen Fraser, National Research Council Canada
Keith Vertanen, Michigan Technological University
Lani Mathew, Mar Baselios College of Engineering and Technology
Natalia Kuzminykh, University of Siena
Ornella Mich, Fondazione Bruno Kessler
Peter Ljunglöf, Chalmers University of Technology
Rachid Riad, Ecole Normale Superieure
Rosalee Wolfe, College of Computing and Digital Media, DePaul University
Simon Judge, University of Sheffield
Zeerak Talat, Simon Fraser University
Zoey Liu, Boston College

Invited Speakers

Annalu Waller, University of Dundee
Raja Kushalnagar, Gallaudet University

Table of Contents

Program

Friday, May 27, 2022

09:00 - 09:30	*Opening Remarks*
09:30 - 10:30	*Keynote 1 (Annalu Waller)*
10:30 - 11:00	*Break*
11:00 - 12:30	*Session 1*
	Applying the Stereotype Content Model to assess disability bias in popular pre-trained NLP models underlying AI-based assistive technologies Brienna Herold, James Waller and Raja Kushalnagar
	A comparison study on patient-psychologist voice diarization Rachid Riad, Hadrien Titeux, Laurie Lemoine, Justine Montillot, Agnes Sliwinski, Jennifer Bagnou, Xuan Cao, Anne-Catherine Bachoud-Levi and Emmanuel Dupoux
	ColorCode: A Bayesian Approach to Augmentative and Alternative Communication with Two Buttons Matthew Daly
12:30 - 14:00	*Break*
14:00 - 14:15	*Poster pitches*
14:15 - 15:15	*Poster session*
15:15 - 16:00	*Break*
16:00 - 16:30	*Session 2*
	On the Ethical Considerations of Text Simplification Sian Gooding
16:30 - 17:30	*Keynote 2 (Raja Kushalnagar)*
17:30 - 18:00	*Closing Remarks*

Design principles of an open-source language modeling microservice package for AAC text-entry applications

Brian Roark
Google Research, US
roark@google.com

Alexander Gutkin
Google Research, UK
agutkin@google.com

Abstract

We present MozoLM, an open-source language model microservice package intended for use in AAC text-entry applications, with a particular focus on the design principles of the library. The intent of the library is to allow the ensembling of multiple diverse language models without requiring the clients (user interface designers, system users or speech-language pathologists) to attend to the formats of the models. Issues around privacy, security, dynamic versus static models, and methods of model combination are explored and specific design choices motivated. Some simulation experiments demonstrating the benefits of personalized language model ensembling via the library are presented.

1 Introduction

Designing and building text-entry systems for individuals with severe motor impairments is a key challenge in the field of augmentative and alternative communication (AAC). In successful cases this typically involves people with many diverse areas of expertise, including speech-language pathologists, those with human-computer interaction (HCI) or natural language processing (NLP) expertise, and, of course, users of the technology themselves. Given this diversity, few individuals will have the breadth of expertise to address all of the issues at play. For example, those focused on interface design or customization for a specific individual's needs may not have the NLP expertise to assemble effective predictive models to help drive the interface; and those who are building state-of-the-art language models (LMs) often lack HCI or AAC experience and are not optimizing their models with text-entry scenarios in mind. As we will illustrate later in the paper, choices of how a system employs LMs can make a big difference in the quality of the resulting predictions, thus effective LM services are critical for these systems. This paper presents the MozoLM open-source software library[1] for building services that allow user interfaces (UIs) to request probabilities from a collection of diverse LMs without having to match their requests to the formats of the models. This frees those working on interfaces and user configuration optimization from having to focus on specific LM details, and frees those working on LMs from necessarily focusing on UI or text-entry scenario specifics.

This work was initially inspired by our interest in Dasher (Ward et al., 2000, 2002), a text-entry system that in its standard implementation[2] is closely tied to certain dynamic language modeling methods (see Section 2 for details).[3] The dynamic nature of the models in Dasher have the virtue of automatically adapting to user input in an open-vocabulary manner, thus learning the idiosyncrasies of the individual over time; however the tight coupling between the modeling choice and interface has some serious drawbacks. First, Dasher could make use of large static general background LMs in addition to user-specific dynamic LMs, to provide extra predictive power for novices with little personalized text but also for more advanced users. This was demonstrated in Rough et al. (2014), who included a static word-based n-gram model in Dasher; we also provide evidence of the benefit of using ensembled static and dynamic LMs later in the paper. Second, Dasher may not be the only text-entry system that an individual makes use of, yet the personalized models maintained by the Dasher system are not straightforwardly accessible to these other applications. Finally, the tight coupling between modeling and the interface requires UI designers to take into account the specifics of the LM and those interested in improving the LMs must attend to the interface. Ideally, a text-entry application should be able to plug in any and all given LMs to derive whatever

[1] https://github.com/google-research/mozolm/
[2] https://www.inference.org.uk/dasher/
[3] MozoLM started as part of work on a new Dasher version.

Ninth Workshop on Speech and Language Processing for Assistive Technologies (SLPAT-2022), pages 1 - 16
May 27, 2022 ©2022 Association for Computational Linguistics

useful information they can, even when all of the models are trained completely independently.

The design of the library was motivated by several considerations. First, large, possibly remote, general purpose LMs and small(er), local personalized models can profitably work in tandem to support open-vocabulary applications, and this is a potentially complex coordination that likely falls outside what many of those contributing to such an application design are interested in developing the expertise to perform. The library should allow for easy-to-configure support of these best practices. Section 3.1 presents the language model design criteria for the library. Second, personalized models must remain secure due to privacy concerns, so such services must include adequate security and privacy functionality. Further, multiple applications could potentially share the same microservice – either multiple text-entry applications on the same local device (hence possibly sharing dynamic models) or many clients for remotely running hubs. Finally, separation of the language modeling functionality into a completely separate component allows for independent development and testing. Such general architectural considerations are presented in Section 3.2.

2 Background

2.1 Language modeling intro and notation

Language models are used to determine the probability of a string S of discrete tokens t drawn from a vocabulary Σ. For ease of notation, let $S = t_0 t_1 t_2 \ldots t_k$ where $t_i \in \Sigma$ for all i. By convention, without loss of generality, let the initial token t_0 always be a special start-of-string token <B> and the final token t_k always be a special end-of-string token <E>. For a given token t_i, let h_i be the history at that position, i.e., the tokens in S prior to t_i which are $t_0 \ldots t_{i-1}$. Then, by the chain rule,

$$P(S) = \prod_{i=1}^{k} P(t_i \mid h_i) .$$

Language models can vary in what they consider a token (e.g., words or characters), what is present in their vocabulary Σ, and in the methods used to estimate $P(t_i \mid h_i)$ at each position in the string[4], but the above formulation holds in general. To provide probabilities, the model must be appropriately normalized so that, for any given history h

$$\sum_{t \in \Sigma} P(t \mid h) = 1$$

and for all $t \in \Sigma$, $0 \leq P(t \mid h) \leq 1$. Many if not most models in use today are appropriately smoothed (or regularized) so that for all $t \in \Sigma$ and $h \in \Sigma^*$, $0 < P(t \mid h) < 1$, i.e., all vocabulary items have non-zero probability in all contexts. Any token that is not found within the vocabulary Σ is called out-of-vocabulary (OOV) and receives zero probability from the model without some additional mechanism to allocate probability to OOVs.

Another language modeling concept that is key for text entry applications is whether the model is dynamic or static. **Dynamic** LMs update the model as new text is produced, so that the LM can subsequently provide higher probabilities to sequences that have already been observed, thus *personalizing* the model. Most large LMs, such as those discussed next as well as neural LMs, are **static**, i.e., they are estimated once then probabilities are served without being updated as text is produced.

2.2 Conventional Word-based n-gram LMs

Word-based n-gram models are a common class of LMs that have been widely used for many applications. They are distinguished by the nature of the vocabulary Σ, which is made up of a closed-vocabulary of words, and by methods for defining equivalence classes of histories based on a Markov assumption. The Markov assumption states that given the previous m words (for some value of m) in the history, the probability of a word is conditionally independent of words earlier in the history (Norris, 1998). Operationally, this assumption implies that, for a given token t_i and history h_i

$$P(t_i \mid h_i) = P(t_i \mid t_{i-m} \ldots t_{i-1}) .$$

So, for example, if $m = 2$, then $P(t \mid h)$ can be estimated by only considering the previous 2 words in the history, e.g., if h = "they are under the bathroom", then

$$P(\text{sink} \mid h) = P(\text{sink} \mid \text{the bathroom}) .$$

The most common smoothing (regularization) method for these models relies on "backing off" to lower-order Markov models (i.e., smaller m) in certain circumstances, and using various methods to both decide when to back off and how to allocate the probabilities appropriately when doing so

[4]Some methods assign probabilities to whole sentences without relying on single-token estimates, such as Rosenfeld (1997), but for our purposes, this formulation suffices.

(Katz, 1987; Kneser and Ney, 1995). See Chen and Goodman (1996) for an overview of such methods.

Importantly in the context of text-entry applications, having a closed vocabulary means that words outside of that vocabulary are OOV, hence those words are assigned zero probability, even with backed off probabilities. Further regularizing to provide non-zero probability to words outside of Σ requires incorporation of probabilities from other kinds of language models.

Recent work in neural language modeling has generally emphasized models with tokens defined somewhere between word and character, at the level of multi-character sub-word tokens. For example, byte-pair encoding (Sennrich et al., 2016) or word-pieces (Schuster and Nakajima, 2012) are learned tokenizations that group together frequent character units, resulting in a configurable balance between the size of the vocabulary and the lengths of dependencies being effectively modeled. Models with these tokenizations provide open-vocabulary modeling like character-based models.

2.3 Language Modeling in AAC

Higginbotham et al. (2012) provide a thorough overview of early work on language modeling in AAC, beyond what we have the space to provide here; we refer readers to that paper for more details. Briefly, LMs are used to optimize keyboard layout and to provide word-completion and prediction utilities, among other uses, mirroring (and often pre-dating) similar approaches for mobile text entry. Optimization of the keyboard layout for scanning methods of text entry, whereby rows and columns of text in a grid are highlighted for selection, were extensively investigated by Lesher et al. (1998a) and others, and frequency-driven placement of characters in such systems remains common. Contextual probabilities can be used for disambiguation in ambiguous keyboards, such as the well-known T9 (Grover et al., 1998), where individual keys are assigned multiple possible characters. Optimizing groupings of such symbols and use of LMs for disambiguation are long-standing practices (Lesher et al., 1998b). LMs can also be used for word prediction, whereby full words are predicted either based on prior context or on the prefix of the word that has been typed (or both), and this has been shown to provide substantial reductions in keystrokes required for text entry in an AAC setting (Higginbotham, 1992). Issues around the cognitive load imposed by attending to word predictions in addition to keyboard manipulation cause the speedup to be less than the keystroke savings might suggest, but this remains a standard component in AAC text-entry systems (Higginbotham et al., 2012). LMs have also been used to improve the accuracy of brain-computer interface (BCI) text-entry systems (Oken et al., 2014), much as they are in mobile keyboards for autocorrection in the face of so-called fat-finger errors or for gesture-based input (Kristensson and Zhai, 2004). With the advent of larger, higher quality neural LMs such as GPT-3 (Brown et al., 2020) or T5 (Raffel et al., 2019), higher quality predictions are available to be leveraged for inclusion in such systems, in many of the same ways that they have been over the years.

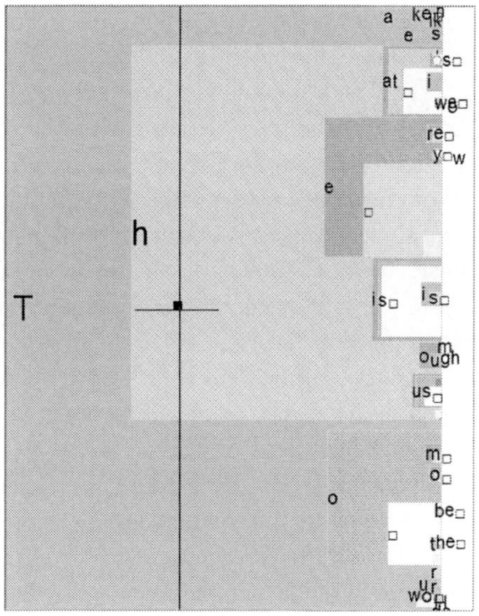

Figure 1: Screenshot of Dasher keyboard.

2.4 Dasher and the PPM Language Model

We will provide some additional details about language modeling in the Dasher system (Ward et al., 2000, 2002; MacKay et al., 2004), both because it provided the initial motivation for the work, but also because the role of the LM in the interface is central (and unique) and the LM focus in Dasher has largely been on dynamic modeling (i.e., personalization), which is particularly important for text-entry applications. A screenshot of the system in operation is shown in Figure 1. Text entry in Dasher is achieved by navigating through an array of characters arranged in lexicographic order. Typing occurs by moving into regions to the right of the screen that are labeled with the intended letter. In the image, the central point has moved past the letters 'T' and 'h' and the most likely next letters (mostly vowels) are associated with relatively large regions, i.e., they are easy targets to navigate into. Word boundaries are marked with the square box, and some predictions extend beyond just the next character. For example, in the image, moving straight to the right of the central dot would result in the continuation "is□is□", corresponding to the (relatively likely) string "This is . . . " Even unlikely continuations have some probability, hence some space allocated to them.

The amount of space allocated for each character is determined by arithmetic coding (Rissanen and Langdon, 1979; Witten et al., 1987), so that high probability characters are larger targets for the navigating user than lower probability characters. Entering text is thus made easier by effective predictions of next characters, via easier-to-hit targets. The letters are arrayed in descending lexicographic order, so that one can move towards a character even if it is too small to see, until that character grows in size as one gets closer. Thus, for example, if one wants to type "Thx" – perhaps as an abbreviation for "Thanks" – then one would navigate towards the bottom of the sorted list. As one navigates in that direction, the probability that the target symbol is found on that end of the list grows, and the regions for those letters grow accordingly. Eventually the region allocated to the character will become large enough to be visible and navigation to that region becomes easier.

These examples illustrate a couple of important considerations for language modeling in Dasher. First, probabilities must be provided for the next character, not just the next word. Second, we may want to type something that does not occur in a standard lexicon, such as "Thx", including things that we may type frequently due to our own personal conventions. Hence personalization, i.e., updating the language model as one types, can lead to higher probabilities for things that an individual frequently types. Due to these considerations, a major component of the Dasher system since the beginning was a dynamic character-based language model, most commonly Prediction by Partial Match or PPM (Cleary and Witten, 1984; Moffat, 1990).[5] See Appendix A.1 for explicit mathematical details of the specific PPM version implemented in MozoLM.

2.5 Microservices in a Nutshell

Before the advent of sophisticated web technologies, such as cloud computing, software architectures were mostly monolithic, consisting of tightly coupled and often overlapping components hosted on the same machine and viewed as a single atomic unit. More often than not, introducing architectural changes to such a system, such as factoring out the data intensive components to run elsewhere or supporting a new platform, required a time-consuming and costly redesign. In recent years a modern alternative paradigm revolving around the notion of *microservices* has gained much popularity and wide acceptance in the industry, well attested by the plethora of books on the subject.[6]

Some of the commonly found definitions of the microservices concept are due to Dragoni et al. (2017) and Zimmermann (2017), who loosely define a microservice architecture as a collection of self-contained distributed services communicating via well-defined APIs, such as remote procedure call (RPC) message passing interfaces. The architecture follows the fine-grained separation of concerns, with each individual service designed around a particular *business capability*. One example may include a hypothetical component focused on user interaction (UI) loosely coupled with an LM component. Developing, testing and maintaining these two components in a microservices architecture can be made possible by two independent cross-functional teams each working in their own area of expertise. The component microservices are *independently deployable*, *scalable*, and *testable*. In our example, adding a new sensory interface to the UI, upgrading the LM or scaling its serving capacity, should not adversely affect the functioning of other components nor require their duplication. The architecture is often *polyglot*, which implies that the development is not restricted to any particular programming language, platform or development stack as long as individual components adhere to the same API for communication. Our implementation is based on popular gRPC high-performance communication framework. See Appendix B for the rationale behind its adoption and the review of such frameworks' use in healthcare.

[5] In addition, Dasher supports the Context Tree Weighting (CTW) method (Willems et al., 1995; Willems, 1998) that was shown to be superior to PPM (van Veen, 2007) but has rarely been used in practical Dasher configurations.

[6] See, e.g. Nadareishvili et al. (2016); Richardson (2019); Newman (2019, 2021); Vernon and Jaskula (2021); Khan et al. (2021); Ziadé and Fraser (2021).

3 Design Considerations

3.1 Language Model Issues

In this section we present general LM issues addressed by the library; further specific language modeling details are provided in Appendix A. A text-entry interface may request probabilities from the LMs given the current context (i.e., what has already been typed), then update the context (and possibly counts of observed strings in dynamic models) as further characters are typed. The interface to LMs should thus focus on two key requests: retrieving probabilities and updating counts/contexts. From the client's perspective, all models are accessed together through a single interface, so these functions must be supported by each model and coordinated by a central "hub". This raises key issues around the coordination of diverse models, including tokenization, static versus dynamic modeling, and methods of ensembling.

Tokenization is a major issue, since LMs are trained variously on different kinds of tokens, from words to sub-words to single characters. For example, the PPM model used in Dasher is a character-based LM, thus providing probabilities over single characters given the context. Large general LMs may be word-based, i.e., providing probabilities over a vocabulary of words, or based on other multi-character sub-word tokens. How does one create an ensemble over models with diverse tokenization? Our approach is to derive the estimates at the smallest unit: single characters, which in the library are defined as single Unicode code points. For a model with multi-character tokens, the probabilities must be calculated by summing the probabilities of all items in the vocabulary that have that character in that context. For example, if the already-typed context is "the dog h", then the probability of a particular letter following 'h' (say 'o') would be the sum of the probabilities of all words in the vocabulary beginning with 'ho' (house, home, hound, however, etc.) following the context 'the dog', appropriately normalized. Similar calculations must happen for sub-word models, so that all models being ensembled within the hub provide single character probabilities. If the UI requires multi-character estimates, e.g., for word prediction or completion, then some additional computation would be required to build them up from single characters. Note that whitespace is a character as well in this approach. Word-based models typically include whitespace implicitly at word boundaries, which must be accounted for.

The software library is built so that a given model type can be defined as a sub-class of the general LM class. Each sub-class must define its version of a set of core functions, such as returning probabilities given a context, returning a new context identifier given a previous context identifier and a newly typed character, and updating the model when characters are typed. Specific sub-classes will have different processing requirements to satisfy these core requests, including summing over multi-character tokens if the model has such a tokenization (as described above), normalizing the probabilities if the model stores raw counts, or actually updating counts in dynamic models. Appendix A.3 presents the model classes that have already been implemented in the MozoLM library.

Different models may provide probabilities for distinct vocabularies of characters, and the ensemble provides probabilities for the union of the model character vocabularies. For example, a local personalized LM P may have never used an accented vowel such as 'é', while a background LM Q would perhaps give that character non-zero probability, having observed it in a large corpus. Since P does not include the character in its vocabulary, its contribution to the overall probability of the character is zero, and all the probability mass for that character must come from Q. The union of all of the model vocabularies will have at least some probability mass coming from some of the models. The LM hub collects the probabilities over single characters from each model, and takes the union in the ensembling process, before returning the results to the client.

Dynamic models must be updated when text is entered, and it is the responsibility of the interface to call the update function. The hub tracks whether models are static or dynamic, and only dynamic models are updated. Dynamic models like the PPM will typically store raw counts and normalize on-the-fly to yield probabilities, while static models can pre-compute normalized probabilities.

Ensembling methods are defined at the hub level and can involve relatively simple approaches, such as interpolation with fixed weights, or more complicated ones that keep track of recent model performance on typed text to determine which model to rely upon. The hub is responsible for determining the mixing weights and ensuring that the final mixture is properly normalized – see Appendix A.2

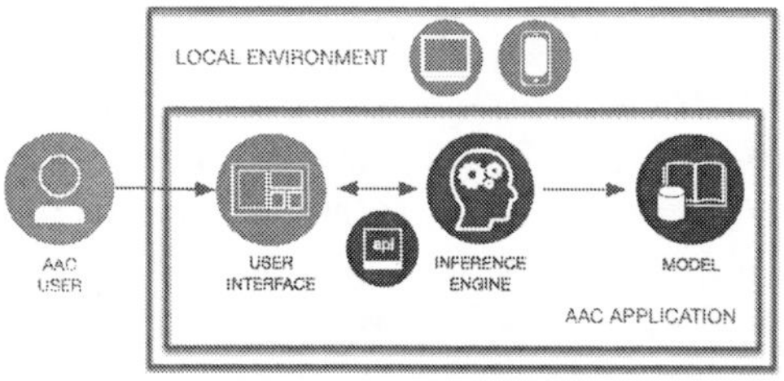

Figure 2: Monolithic AAC text-entry architecture.

for methods available in the library.

Many modeling methods require some extra processing to provide normalized character-level probabilities upon request at a given context, so it may be useful to cache the values for a context, to handle repeated visits more efficiently. This introduces a speed/memory tradeoff, and this tradeoff is generally handled at the LM sub-class level, since each modeling method may need to cache different information. For example, word-based n-gram models must sum over tokens to derive character-level estimates, and some information may be cached to make such summing more efficient. Again, see Appendix A.3 for details.

3.2 Architecture Details

AAC text-entry systems are commonly structured as a monolith compiled into a single application, shown schematically in Figure 2, where the system's tightly coupled components are crudely divided into a UI, an inference engine and an LM. The UI is often a complex system on its own, typically integrating various modes of user control, such as gaze tracking, and display. The inference engine is responsible for querying the supported LM and translating the LM estimates into a representation anticipated by the UI.

Separation of Concerns with LM Hub Splitting the business logic into interaction with the UI and display on the one hand, and LMs on the other, provides several advantages over the monolithic design. Consider the architecture in Figure 3 which shows a microservices configuration consisting of two components hosted on the same device. The main difference from the monolithic configuration in Figure 2 is that all the functionality that deals with LM inference now resides in a separated local service – the LM hub. What is left in the AAC application is a thin inter-process communication (IPC) layer for communicating with the LM hub using a gRPC UNIX socket mechanism (Stevens and Rago, 2013).

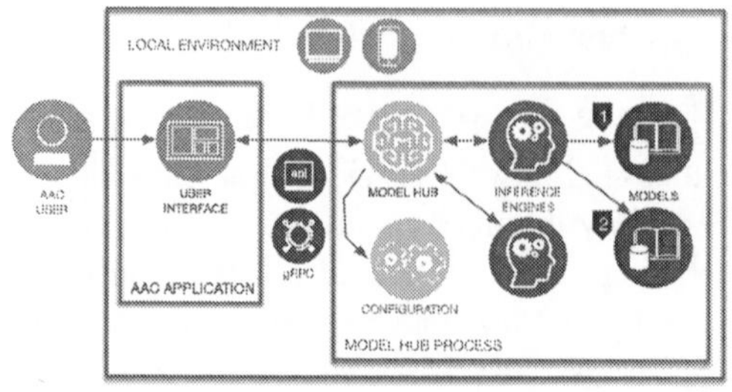

Figure 3: Monolith split into the UI and the LM hub.

In a typical scenario we envisage the LM hub as a standalone service binary that runs as a separate process from the UI application if on the same device, and as a remote gRPC service if configured to run over the network. Alternatively, the LM hub is also available as a regular library, which still allows the developer to combine the UI and LM components into a single monolith, simply a better structured one. The additional advantage of this architecture (mentioned in Section 2) is that it is "polyglot", e.g., the AAC application may be implemented in C++, while the LM hub may be implemented in Swift for accessing the native Apple iOS keyboard predictions (Ruan et al., 2018).

LM Hub Structure The primary purpose of the model hub service is to provide the LM predictions from one or several inference engines based on the service configuration (Appendix C.1 describes the configuration language). The inference engine is an abstraction that implements the model serving logic for particular types of model. The local architecture in Figure 3 has two model inference engines. The first engine serves two models. This inference engine implements light-weight dynamic LMs (models 1 and 2 in the figure) with the individual model predictions served by this engine combined by the model hub using a mixture method such as one of those presented in Appendix A. The second inference engine may serve bigger static LMs, such as pruned n-gram LMs (Heafield, 2011; Roark et al., 2012). Alternatively, this inference engine may serve a distilled neural model (Jiao et al., 2020; Sun et al., 2020; Niu et al., 2020). In either case the static model is optimized for running on an edge device.

Distributed LM Hubs Because in the proposed architecture the model hub is an independently deployable service, building a fully distributed architecture, where the model hub runs as a remote service, becomes easy. Figure 4 shows two of the

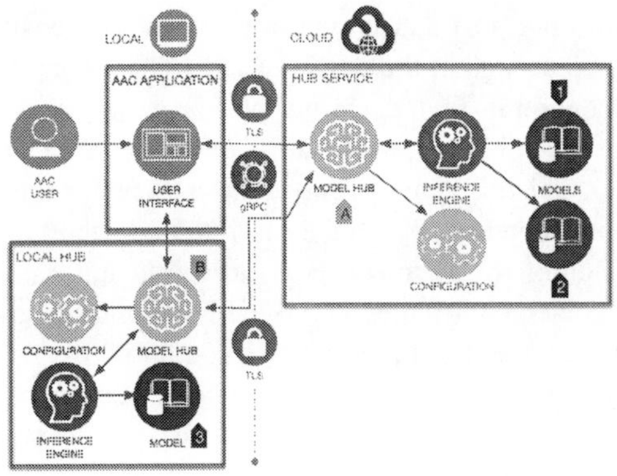

Figure 4: Architecture with a local and remote LM hubs in two configurations: a remote hub (A) only, and a local hub (B) communicating with the remote hub.

simplest distributed configurations possible.

The first scenario involves a single remote model hub service (denoted A in the figure). In our example this hub is virtually identical to the local in-process hub from Figure 3 in that it also serves two models. The main difference, of course, is that the models served by the remote hub may be chosen to be static rather than dynamic for a number of reasons, e.g., related to privacy (remote machine may not be fully trusted with user data) or computation (the machine may be powerful enough to serve large unoptimized models). Another important difference is that the communication between the AAC application and the model hub uses network gRPC channel secured using standard authentication mechanism, such as transport layer security (TLS) protocol (IETF, 2018). More implementation details are provided in Appendix C.2.

The second scenario in Figure 4 involves a distributed dual hub architecture: the AAC application communicates with a local model hub service (denoted B in the figure), which in turn communicates with the remote LM hub service (A) described above. The design feature that allows each LM hub to act as a client for other LM hubs enables more sophisticated architectures such as the one we are describing. In this example, the local hub is serving a single dynamic model, while the remote hub may be providing predictions from two third-party static models, with model ensembling being performed by each hub. Even more complex architectures are supported (see Appendix D).

4 Personalization Experiment

We have motivated this work in part with the idea that LMs with different characteristics can be profitably ensembled to provide better estimates, and in this section we present a small experiment to demonstrate this. This experiment was run using the MozoLM library with differently configured LM hubs and implementations of several common LM sub-classes.[7] We evaluated LM performance using data from the Enron Personalization Validation Set[8] (Fowler et al., 2015). That data collects emails written by 89 individuals, each in their own separate file, 45 of which are available for dev and 44 for test. Here we use the text from the 45 dev individuals, found in files `dev??.message.text.tsv`, up to a maximum of 140,000 characters per individual, in aggregate over 720k words and 3.9M characters.

Language models can be used for any number of applications – including text entry, the focus of this software library – but evaluation of language model quality is often performed intrinsically, by examining the probabilities assigned by models to attested text from the domain. Operationally, one measures the log probability of the validation corpus; and for ease of comparison at the character level, normalizes by the number of characters. If the log is base 2, this provides the number of bits per character (BPC), and lower values correspond to higher probabilities, i.e., better models.

Since each file in the dev set consists of text written by a single individual, dynamic models that update counts as the text file is processed will personalize the model to predict frequent patterns of that particular user. We score the cumulative BPC of the model, which, at each character, shows us how well the model has predicted the text that was typed up to that point. Lower BPC corresponds to higher probability assigned to the actual characters that were typed, i.e., better predictions of what the user will type. In Dasher, for example, this would correspond to larger regions being allocated to actual target characters within its arithmetic coding approach. Since we measure cumulative BPC at each character position, we can track the learning of any dynamic models that are included in the ensemble.

Figure 5 presents cumulative BPC aggregated over all 45 individuals in the dev partition, reporting the aggregate bits divided by aggregate characters as we synchronously step through each text

[7]The data used to train models is available at https://github.com/agutkin/slpat2022.

[8]https://github.com/google-research-datasets/EnronPersonalizationValidation

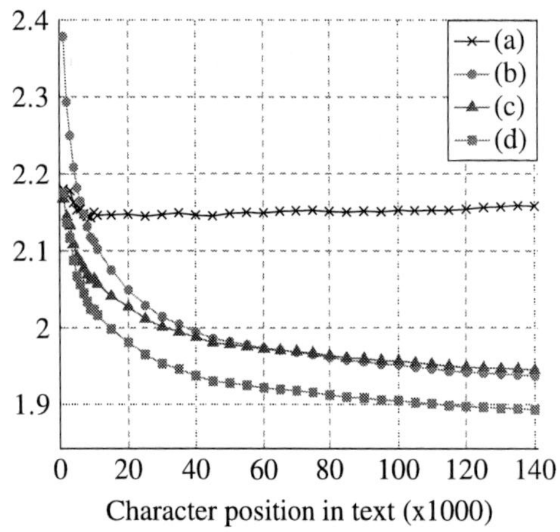

Figure 5: Cumulative BPC at text positions in collections of emails by the same individual, in four conditions: (a) uniformly-mixed ensemble of two static LMs; (b) uniformly-mixed ensemble of the two static models and a dynamic PPM 6-gram for each individual; and (c) and (d) Bayesian-mixed ensembles of the two static models and a dynamic PPM 6-gram for each individual, using history lengths 6 and 1, respectively, to determine mixing coefficients.

file. Thus, at position 5000, the cumulative BPC shows that measure for all users up to and including character 5000 in each of the files. Note that the dynamic LMs are being updated only for the specific individual, not shared among individuals.

Figure 5 presents cumulative BPC for four conditions. First, we combined two large static LMs trained on 20M sentences of English Wikipedia text (426M words). The first is a trigram word model with a closed vocabulary of 414,715 words; all other words are mapped to an out-of-vocabulary (OOV) token. This model was built using the OpenGrm NGram library (Roark et al., 2012) and pruned to contain a total of 100M n-grams. The second static model is an unpruned PPM model with a maximum n-gram length of 6, trained on the same data. Since this is a character-level model, the ensembling of these two models provides a fully open-vocabulary model over the characters found in the Wikipedia training data, and there are no OOV characters in the evaluation text. Condition (a) in Figure 5 shows the performance of an ensemble of the two static models, mixed uniformly. Note that this yields lower BPC (i.e., better performance) than using either model independently, conditions which are not shown for clarity.

The other three conditions mix the above static models with a dynamic PPM model (also maximum 6-gram) that is only trained on previously typed strings in the dev set itself. This dynamic model on its own performs far worse than any of the ensembles shown (results are omitted for clarity). The difference between these three dynamic model conditions is in the ensembling method. In condition (b), all three models are mixed uniformly, i.e., each contributes 1/3 of the probability mass. One can see from Figure 5 that condition (b) ends up improving substantially over condition (a), but at early character positions (b) has significantly higher BPC, since the dynamic model needs many observations before it can begin to produce useful probabilities. The other two conditions use a generalization of Bayesian interpolation (see Appendix A.2) to establish the ensemble mixing coefficients, which, among other things, reduces reliance on the dynamic model at earlier positions. Choosing the mixing coefficients based on just the previously typed character (condition d) outperforms using the previous 6 typed characters to calculate the coefficients (condition c).

This experiment is simply intended to motivate the ensembling of multiple diverse models, as we advocate for in the design of this library, as well as demonstrating the software in action. Of course, actual optimal model configuration will depend on the user and on the specific text-entry system being used. We can at least say that different models can have complementary characteristics, so that combining them, even in simple ways, can yield better models.

5 Conclusion and Future Work

We have presented the rationale for many choices made in designing an open-source microservice package for language modeling in AAC text-entry applications. The code presented is available open-source, and the experiments run in Section 4 were performed using the library. Future work will include adding more LM sub-classes, including commonly used neural LMs.

Acknowledgements

Thanks to Keith Vertanen, Jim Hawkins, Jeremy Cope, Will Wade, Jay Beavers, Stefan Zecevic, Lisie Lillianfeld and Jiban Adhikary for sharing their insights and expertise with us during the work on this project. The authors also thank Richard Sproat and the three anonymous reviewers for their useful feedback on the earlier version of this paper.

References

Randy Abernethy. 2019. *Programmer's Guide to Apache Thrift*. Manning Publications Co., Shelter Island, NY, USA.

Rami Al-Rfou, Dokook Choe, Noah Constant, Mandy Guo, and Llion Jones. 2019. Character-level language modeling with deeper self-attention. In *Proceedings of the 33rd AAAI conference on Artificial Intelligence*, pages 3159–3166, Honolulu, Hawaii, USA. ACM.

Cyril Allauzen and Michael Riley. 2011. Bayesian language model interpolation for mobile speech input. In *Proceedings of Interspeech*, pages 1429–1432, Florence, Italy. International Speech Communication Association (ISCA).

Adam Berger, Stephen A. Della Pietra, and Vincent J. Della Pietra. 1996. A maximum entropy approach to natural language processing. *Computational Linguistics*, 22(1):39–71.

Tom Brown, Benjamin Mann, Nick Ryder, Melanie Subbiah, Jared D Kaplan, Prafulla Dhariwal, Arvind Neelakantan, Pranav Shyam, Girish Sastry, Amanda Askell, Sandhini Agarwal, Ariel Herbert-Voss, Gretchen Krueger, Tom Henighan, Rewon Child, Aditya Ramesh, Daniel Ziegler, Jeffrey Wu, Clemens Winter, Chris Hesse, Mark Chen, Eric Sigler, Mateusz Litwin, Scott Gray, Benjamin Chess, Jack Clark, Christopher Berner, Sam McCandlish, Alec Radford, Ilya Sutskever, and Dario Amodei. 2020. Language models are few-shot learners. In *Advances in Neural Information Processing Systems*, volume 33, pages 1877–1901. Curran Associates, Inc.

Mauro Caporuscio, Danny Weyns, Jesper Andersson, Clara Axelsson, and Göran Petersson. 2017. IoT-enabled physical telerehabilitation platform. In *2017 IEEE International Conference on Software Architecture Workshops (ICSAW)*, pages 112–119, Gothenburg, Sweden. IEEE.

Stanley F. Chen and Joshua Goodman. 1996. An empirical study of smoothing techniques for language modeling. In *34th Annual Meeting of the Association for Computational Linguistics*, pages 310–318, Santa Cruz, California, USA. Association for Computational Linguistics.

John Cleary and Ian Witten. 1984. Data compression using adaptive coding and partial string matching. *IEEE Transactions on Communications*, 32(4):396–402.

Ciprian Dobre, Lidia Băjenaru, Ion Alexandru Marinescu, Mihaela Tomescu, Gabriel Ioan Prada, and Susanna Spinsante. 2021. New opportunities for older adults care transition from traditional to personalised assistive care: vINCI platform. In *Proceedings of 2021 23rd International Conference on Control Systems and Computer Science (CSCS)*, pages 515–520, Bucharest, Romania. IEEE.

Nicola Dragoni, Saverio Giallorenzo, Alberto Lluch Lafuente, Manuel Mazzara, Fabrizio Montesi, Ruslan Mustafin, and Larisa Safina. 2017. Microservices: Yesterday, today, and tomorrow. *Present and Ulterior Software Engineering*, pages 195–216.

Hicham El Boukkouri, Olivier Ferret, Thomas Lavergne, Hiroshi Noji, Pierre Zweigenbaum, and Jun'ichi Tsujii. 2020. CharacterBERT: Reconciling ELMo and BERT for word-level open-vocabulary representations from characters. In *Proceedings of the 28th International Conference on Computational Linguistics*, pages 6903–6915, Barcelona, Spain (Online). International Committee on Computational Linguistics.

Marius Eriksen. 2014. Your server as a function. *ACM SIGOPS Operating Systems Review*, 48(1):51–57.

Andrew Fowler, Kurt Partridge, Ciprian Chelba, Xiaojun Bi, Tom Ouyang, and Shumin Zhai. 2015. Effects of language modeling and its personalization on touchscreen typing performance. In *Proceedings of the 33rd ACM SIGCHI Conference on Human Factors in Computing Systems*, pages 649–658, Seoul, Korea. ACM.

Dale L. Grover, Martin T. King, and Clifford A. Kushler. 1998. Reduced keyboard disambiguating computer. U.S. Patent US5818437A, October. Tegic Communications Inc.

Kenneth Heafield. 2011. KenLM: Faster and smaller language model queries. In *Proceedings of the Sixth Workshop on Statistical Machine Translation*, pages 187–197, Edinburgh, Scotland. Association for Computational Linguistics.

D. Jeffery Higginbotham. 1992. Evaluation of keystroke savings across five assistive communication technologies. *Augmentative and Alternative Communication*, 8(4):258–272.

D. Jeffery Higginbotham, Gregory W. Lesher, Bryan J. Moulton, and Brian Roark. 2012. The application of natural language processing to augmentative and alternative communication. *Assistive Technology*, 24(1):14–24.

Paul Glor Howard. 1993. *The design and analysis of efficient lossless data compression systems*. Ph.D. thesis, Department of Computer Science, Brown University, Providence, RI, USA. Tech. Report No. CS-93-28.

Bo-June Hsu. 2007. Generalized linear interpolation of language models. In *Proceedings of IEEE Workshop on Automatic Speech Recognition & Understanding (ASRU)*, pages 136–140, Kyoto, Japan. IEEE.

Joshua Humphries, David Konsumer, David Muto, Robert Ross, and Carles Sistare. 2018. *Practical gRPC*. Bleeding Edge Press, Santa Rosa, CA, USA.

IETF. 2018. The transport layer security (TLS) protocol version 1.3. Internet Engineering Task Force, RFC 8446. Version 1.3, August.

Kasun Indrasiri and Danesh Kuruppu. 2020. *gRPC Up & Running: Building Cloud Native Applications with Go and Java for Docker and Kubernetes*. O'Reilly Media, Inc., USA.

Frederick Jelinek and R. L. Mercer. 1980. Interpolated estimation of Markov source parameters from sparse data. In *Proceedings of Workshop on Pattern Recognition in Practice*, pages 381–397, Amsterdam, The Netherlands. North-Holland Publishing.

Xiaoqi Jiao, Yichun Yin, Lifeng Shang, Xin Jiang, Xiao Chen, Linlin Li, Fang Wang, and Qun Liu. 2020. TinyBERT: Distilling BERT for natural language understanding. In *Findings of the Association for Computational Linguistics: EMNLP 2020*, pages 4163–4174, Online. Association for Computational Linguistics.

Simon Josefsson and Sean Leonard. 2015. Textual encodings of PKIX, PKCS, and CMS structures. Internet Engineering Task Force (IETF), RFC 7468. April.

Slava Katz. 1987. Estimation of probabilities from sparse data for the language model component of a speech recognizer. *IEEE transactions on acoustics, speech, and signal processing*, 35(3):400–401.

Ovais Mehboob Ahmed Khan, Arvind Chandaka, and Robert Vettor. 2021. *Developing Microservices Architecture on Microsoft Azure with Open Source Technologies*. Microsoft Press.

Dietrich Klakow. 1998. Log-linear interpolation of language models. In *Proceedings of the 5th International Conference on Spoken Language Processing (ICSLP)*, page paper 0522, Sydney, Australia. International Speech Communication Association (ISCA).

Reinhard Kneser and Hermann Ney. 1995. Improved backing-off for m-gram language modeling. In *Proceedings of the 1995 International Conference on Acoustics, Speech, and Signal Processing (ICASSP)*, volume 1, pages 181–184, Detroit, Michigan, USA. IEEE.

Per-Ola Kristensson and Shumin Zhai. 2004. SHARK^2: a large vocabulary shorthand writing system for pen-based computers. In *Proceedings of the 17th annual ACM symposium on User Interface Software and Technology (UIST)*, pages 43–52, Santa Fe, NM, USA. Association for Computing Machinery (ACM).

Gregory Lesher, Bryan Moulton, and D. Jeffery Higginbotham. 1998a. Techniques for augmenting scanning communication. *Augmentative and Alternative Communication*, 14(2):81–101.

Gregory W. Lesher, Bryan J. Moulton, and D. Jeffery Higginbotham. 1998b. Optimal character arrangements for ambiguous keyboards. *IEEE Transactions on Rehabilitation Engineering*, 6(4):415–423.

Xunying Liu, Mark John Francis Gales, and Philip C. Woodland. 2013. Use of contexts in language model interpolation and adaptation. *Computer Speech & Language*, 27(1):301–321.

David J. C. MacKay, Chris J. Ball, and Mick Donegan. 2004. Efficient communication with one or two buttons. *AIP Conference Proceedings*, 735(1):207–218.

Argyro Mavrogiorgou, Spyridon Kleftakis, Konstantinos Mavrogiorgos, Nikolaos Zafeiropoulos, Andreas Menychtas, Athanasios Kiourtis, Ilias Maglogiannis, and Dimosthenis Kyriazis. 2021. beHEALTHIER: A microservices platform for analyzing and exploiting healthcare data. In *Proceedings of IEEE 34th International Symposium on Computer-Based Medical Systems (CBMS)*, pages 283–288, Aveiro, Portugal. IEEE.

Andrea Melis, Silvia Mirri, Catia Prandi, Marco Prandini, Paola Salomoni, and Franco Callegati. 2016. A microservice architecture use case for persons with disabilities. In *Proceedings of 2nd International Conference on Smart Objects and Technologies for Social Good (GOODTECHS)*, pages 41–50, Venice, Italy. Springer.

Russ Miles and Kim Hamilton. 2006. *Learning UML 2.0: A Pragmatic Introduction to UML*. O'Reilly Media, Inc., USA.

Alistair Moffat. 1990. Implementing the PPM data compression scheme. *IEEE Transactions on Communications*, 38(11):1917–1921.

Mukhriddin Mukhiddinov and Jinsoo Cho. 2021. Smart glass system using deep learning for the blind and visually impaired. *Electronics*, 10(22):2756.

Irakli Nadareishvili, Ronnie Mitra, Matt McLarty, and Mike Amundsen. 2016. *Microservice Architecture: Aligning Principles, Practices, and Culture*. O'Reilly Media, Inc., USA.

Sam Newman. 2019. *Monolith to Microservices: Evolutionary Patterns to Transform Your Monolith*. O'Reilly Media, Inc., USA.

Sam Newman. 2021. *Building Microservices: Designing Fine-Grained Systems*, 2nd edition. O'Reilly Media, Inc., USA.

Wei Niu, Zhenglun Kong, Geng Yuan, Weiwen Jiang, Jiexiong Guan, Caiwen Ding, Pu Zhao, Sijia Liu, Bin Ren, and Yanzhi Wang. 2020. Real-time execution of large-scale language models on mobile. *arXiv preprint arXiv:2009.06823*.

James Robert Norris. 1998. *Markov Chains*. Number 2 in Cambridge Series in Statistical and Probabilistic Mathematics. Cambridge University Press, Cambridge, UK.

Barry S. Oken, Umut Orhan, Brian Roark, Deniz Erdogmus, Andrew Fowler, Aimee Mooney, Betts Peters, Meghan Miller, and Melanie B. Fried-Oken.

2014. Brain–computer interface with language model–electroencephalography fusion for locked-in syndrome. *Neurorehabilitation and Neural Repair*, 28(4):387–394.

Adina M. Panchea, Dominic Létourneau, Simon Brière, Mathieu Hamel, Marc-Antoine Maheux, Cédric Godin, Michel Tousignant, Mathieu Labbé, François Ferland, François Grondin, and François Michaud. 2021. OpenTera: A microservice architecture solution for rapid prototyping of robotic solutions to COVID-19 challenges in care facilities. *arXiv preprint arXiv:2103.06171*.

Anelis Pereira-Vale, Eduardo B Fernandez, Raúl Monge, Hernán Astudillo, and Gastón Márquez. 2021. Security in microservice-based systems: A multivocal literature review. *Computers & Security*, 103:102200.

Gabriela Postolache, Pedro Silva Girão, Octavian Adrian Postolache, José Miguel Dias Pereira, and Vitor Viegas. 2019. IoT based model of healthcare for physiotherapy. In *Proceedings of 2019 13th International Conference on Sensing Technology (ICST)*, pages 1–6, Sydney, Australia. IEEE.

Colin Raffel, Noam Shazeer, Adam Roberts, Katherine Lee, Sharan Narang, Michael Matena, Yanqi Zhou, Wei Li, and Peter J Liu. 2019. Exploring the limits of transfer learning with a unified text-to-text transformer. *arXiv preprint arXiv:1910.10683*.

Krzysztof Rakowski. 2015. *Learning Apache Thrift*. Packt Publishing, Birmingham, UK.

Jorge Rendulich, Jorge R. Beingolea, Milagros Zegarra, Isaac G. G. Vizcarra, and Sergio T. Kofuji. 2019. An IoT environment for the development of assistive applications in smart cities. In *Proceedings of 2019 IEEE 1st Sustainable Cities Latin America Conference (SCLA)*, pages 1–4, Arequipa, Peru. IEEE.

Chris Richardson. 2019. *Microservices Patterns: With examples in Java*. Manning Publications Co., Shelter Island, NY, USA.

Jorma Rissanen and Glen G. Langdon. 1979. Arithmetic coding. *IBM Journal of Research and Development*, 23(2):149–162.

Brian Roark, Richard Sproat, Cyril Allauzen, Michael Riley, Jeffrey Sorensen, and Terry Tai. 2012. The OpenGrm open-source finite-state grammar software libraries. In *Proceedings of the ACL 2012 System Demonstrations*, pages 61–66, Jeju Island, Korea. Association for Computational Linguistics.

Ronald Rosenfeld. 1997. A whole sentence maximum entropy language model. In *Proceedings of the IEEE Workshop on Automatic Speech Recognition and Understanding (ASRU)*, pages 230–237, Santa Barbara, CA, USA. IEEE.

Daniel Rough, Keith Vertanen, and Per Ola Kristensson. 2014. An evaluation of Dasher with a high-performance language model as a gaze communication method. In *Proceedings of the 2014 International Working Conference on Advanced Visual Interfaces*, pages 169–176, Como, Italy. Association for Computing Machinery (ACM).

Sherry Ruan, Jacob O. Wobbrock, Kenny Liou, Andrew Ng, and James A. Landay. 2018. Comparing speech and keyboard text entry for short messages in two languages on touchscreen phones. *Proceedings of the ACM on Interactive, Mobile, Wearable and Ubiquitous Technologies*, 1(4):1–23.

Mike Schuster and Kaisuke Nakajima. 2012. Japanese and Korean voice search. In *Proceedings of 2012 IEEE International Conference on Acoustics, Speech and Signal Processing (ICASSP)*, pages 5149–5152, Kyoto, Japan. IEEE.

Rico Sennrich, Barry Haddow, and Alexandra Birch. 2016. Neural machine translation of rare words with subword units. In *Proceedings of the 54th Annual Meeting of the Association for Computational Linguistics (Volume 1: Long Papers)*, pages 1715–1725, Berlin, Germany. Association for Computational Linguistics.

Christian Steinruecken, Zoubin Ghahramani, and David MacKay. 2015. Improving PPM with dynamic parameter updates. In *Proceedings of 2015 Data Compression Conference (DCC)*, pages 193–202, Snowbird, Utah, USA. IEEE.

W. Richard Stevens and Stephen A. Rago. 2013. *Advanced Programming in the UNIX® Environment*, 3rd edition. Addison-Wesley Professional Computing Series. Addison-Wesley.

Zhiqing Sun, Hongkun Yu, Xiaodan Song, Renjie Liu, Yiming Yang, and Denny Zhou. 2020. MobileBERT: a compact task-agnostic BERT for resource-limited devices. In *Proceedings of the 58th Annual Meeting of the Association for Computational Linguistics*, pages 2158–2170, Online. Association for Computational Linguistics.

Martijn van Veen. 2007. Using context-tree weighting as a language modeler in Dasher. Master's thesis, Department of Electrical Engineering, Eindhoven University of Technology, Eindhoven, The Netherlands, February.

Vaughn Vernon and Tomasz Jaskula. 2021. *Strategic Monoliths and Microservices: Driving Innovation Using Purposeful Architecture*. Pearson Addison-Wesley Signature Series. Addison-Wesley Professional.

David J. Ward. 2001. *Adaptive Computer Interfaces*. Ph.D. thesis, Inference Group, Cavendish Laboratory, University of Cambridge, Cambridge, UK.

David J. Ward, Alan F. Blackwell, and David J. C. MacKay. 2000. Dasher — a data entry interface using continuous gestures and language models. In *Proceedings of the 13th annual ACM symposium on User Interface Software and Technology (UIST)*, pages 129–137, San Diego, California, USA. Association for Computing Machinery (ACM).

David J. Ward, Alan F. Blackwell, and David J. C. MacKay. 2002. Dasher: A gesture-driven data entry interface for mobile computing. *Human–Computer Interaction*, 17(2-3):199–228.

Frans M. J. Willems. 1998. The context-tree weighting method: Extensions. *IEEE Transactions on Information Theory*, 44(2):792–798.

Frans M. J. Willems, Yuri M. Shtarkov, and Tjalling J. Tjalkens. 1995. The context-tree weighting method: Basic properties. *IEEE Transactions on Information Theory*, 41(3):653–664.

Edwin B. Wilson. 1927. Probable inference, the law of succession, and statistical inference. *Journal of the American Statistical Association*, 22(158):209–212.

Ian H. Witten, Radford M. Neal, and John G. Cleary. 1987. Arithmetic coding for data compression. *Communications of the ACM*, 30(6):520–540.

Zhilin Yang, Zihang Dai, Yiming Yang, Jaime Carbonell, Russ R Salakhutdinov, and Quoc V Le. 2019. XLNet: Generalized autoregressive pretraining for language understanding. In *Advances in Neural Information Processing Systems (NeurIPS)*, volume 32. Curran Associates, Inc.

Tetiana Yarygina. 2018. *Exploring Microservice Security*. Ph.D. thesis, Department of Informatics, University of Bergen, Bergen, Norway.

Yeliz Yesilada and Simon Harper. 2019. Futurama. In Yeliz Yesilada and Simon Harper, editors, *Web Accessibility: A Foundation for Research*, 2nd edition, Human–Computer Interaction Series, pages 791–803. Springer, London, UK.

Tarek Ziadé and Simon Fraser. 2021. *Python Microservices Development: Build efficient and lightweight microservices using the Python tooling ecosystem*, 2nd edition. Packt Publishing, Birmingham, UK.

Olaf Zimmermann. 2017. Microservices tenets: Agile approach to service development and deployment. *Computer Science — Research and Development*, 32(3):301–310.

A Language Modeling Specifics

A.1 PPM Language Model

There are many PPM variants – see Ward (2001) for a review. Here we will present the PPMD variant (Howard, 1993) that has been implemented in this library. We follow the "blending" and "update exclusion" (known as *single counting* from Moffat, 1990) approach taken in Steinruecken et al. (2015), and assign probabilities using a variant of equation 4 in that paper. In such an approach, there are three hyperparameters: α, β and m. Both α and β fall between 0 and 1, and $m \geq 0$ specifies that the longest strings included in the model are of length $m \quad 1$.

Let Σ be a vocabulary of characters, including a special end-of-string symbol. Let $h \in \Sigma^*$ be the contextual history and $t \in \Sigma$ a token following h, e.g., h might be "this is the contextual histor" and t might be "y". Let h' be the back-off contextual history for h, which is the longest proper suffix of h if one exists, and the empty string otherwise. Thus, for our example above, h' is "his is the contextual histor". For any $x \in \Sigma^*$ let $c(x)$ denote the count of x, and $C(x) = \max(c(x) - \beta, 0)$. We will specify how counts are derived later. Finally, let $U(h) = \{t : c(ht) > 0\}$ and $S(h) = \sum_x c(hx)$.

Probabilities are defined based on "blending" multiple orders, a calculation which recurses to lower orders, terminating at the unigram probability, which is when h is the empty string. For the unigram probability, we smooth via add-one Laplace smoothing (Wilson, 1927), i.e., for all $t \in \Sigma$

$$P(t) = \frac{c(t) \quad 1}{\sum_x c(x) \quad 1}.$$

If h is non-empty, then its probability is defined using the metaparameters α, β mentioned earlier:

$$P(t \mid h) = \frac{C(ht) \quad (U(h)\beta \quad \alpha)\, P(t \mid h')}{S(h) \quad \alpha}.$$

Counting occurs via "update exclusion". With each new observation t in the context of h, we update our count $c(ht)$. Let $k = \min(\text{length}(ht), m \quad 1)$, and let $X = h't$ be the suffix of ht of length k. Let X' be the longest suffix of X that was previously observed, i.e., where $c(X') > 0$.[9] Then we increment the counts by one for all substrings Y of ht such that length(X) >= length(Y) >= length(X'). See Steinruecken et al. (2015) for further details about this method.

A.2 Ensembling Methods

Two language models, such as M_1 and M_2 shown in Figure 3, can be combined into an ensemble model in many ways. Perhaps the simplest requires just a single parameter λ between 0 and 1 that determines

[9]We assume that t has been observed, since we use Laplace add-one smoothing for the unigram.

how much of the probability to derive from M_1, with the rest ($1-\lambda$) coming from M_2:

$$P(t \mid h) = \lambda P_1(t \mid h) \quad (1-\lambda)P_2(t \mid h)\,,$$

where P_k is the probability as given by model M_k. This approach can generalize beyond two models by mixing a third model, such as M_3 in the local hub of Figure 4, with the above ensemble using a second mixing parameter γ (also between 0 and 1):

$$\begin{aligned} P(t \mid h) &= \gamma(\lambda P_1(t \mid h) \quad (1-\lambda)P_2(t \mid h)) \\ &\quad (1-\gamma)P_3(t \mid h) \end{aligned}$$

The method of estimating the mixing parameters λ, γ can vary, and includes long-known methods such as using expectation maximization (EM) on a held-aside corpus (Jelinek and Mercer, 1980), which is also used for backoff smoothing parameter estimation in some approaches.

Ensembling can have several benefits in the context of text-entry applications. First, it can allow for the use of closed-vocabulary word-based models without assigning zero probability to OOV words, when mixed with an open-vocabulary, e.g., character-based, model. Second, models trained on different training sets can be complementary in their distributions, so that a mixture of the two provides better overall probabilities than either model on its own. Finally, mixtures of static and dynamic models can provide better personalization than is provided by just dynamic models on their own, as evidenced in the results of Section 4.

For those experiments, we used a somewhat more complicated method (also available in the library) for calculating the mixture than single parameters λ and γ, based on a generalization of Bayesian interpolation (Allauzen and Riley, 2011). Given K models, each $k \in K$ having a normalized prior weight w_k such that $\sum_{k \in K} w_k = 1.0$, then

$$P(t \mid h) = \sum_{k \in K} m_k(h) P_k(t \mid h)\,,$$

where $P_k(t \mid h)$ is the probability of t given h in model k, and $m_k(h)$ is the mixture weight for model k given history h, calculated as

$$m_k(h) = \frac{w_k P_k(h)}{\sum_{k' \in K} w_{k'} P_{k'}(h)}\,.$$

In this version, the length of the history considered when calculating $P_k(h)$ is parameterized, so that we consider only the previous j symbols regardless of the order of the model, where j is a given parameter. For $j > 0$:

$$m_k(h_i) = \frac{1}{Z} w_k P_k(t_{i-1} \mid h_{i-1}) \ldots P_k(t_{i-j} \mid h_{i-j})\,,$$

where Z is the appropriate normalization across all models so that the mixture weights sum to one.

The plot in Figure 5 shows that using this method can effectively balance the use of static and dynamic models so that, before sufficient observations have been accrued in the dynamic model, the static models are relied upon. Using just one previous character to assign the mixtures yielded a better ensemble model than using the prior 6 characters.

In addition to the linear formulation that we've been presenting in this section, more sophisticated types of fixed-weight interpolation exist, including log-linear interpolation (Klakow, 1998) inspired by maximum entropy models (Berger et al., 1996); generalized linear interpolation using context (history)-dependent weights (Hsu, 2007); and the combination of both linear and log-linear methods (Liu et al., 2013).

A.3 Model Classes Implemented in Library

At the current time, four language model subclasses have been defined in the library: a simple bigram character model class using a dense matrix to encode the model; a character n-gram class that uses the OpenGrm NGram model finite-state transducer (FST) format (Roark et al., 2012) to encode the model; a word-based n-gram class also using the OpenGrm FST format; and a PPM model class, also represented internally as a finite-state transducer. The point of the library is to allow the addition of new model classes, and these existing classes provide examples of how to do this for, say, neural language models. In this section, we will briefly identify some of the features of the model classes that were required to make them function within the ensembling framework.

Two of the classes require extra processing to serve the probabilities from the stored model format. First, for the word-based n-gram model, character-level probabilities must be derived by summing over all words that match the history. To do this, we sort the model lexicon in lexicographic order and collect all word probabilities at the word-initial position. Then, as each letter of the current word is typed, all the words that match that prefix fall within an interval in the lexicon. Pre-summing the probabilities over the whole list allows us to calculate the total probability in the interval via a single difference in probabilities. Second, counts are stored in the PPM model, rather than normalized probabilities, since the model is typically dynamic, i.e., it is being updated with new counts as the system operates. For this reason, calculation of probabilities from counts is required before serving probabilities in this model class.

Because both of these models require extra processing, a small bounded caching approach is included in both model classes, to permit states in the model to store calculated results in case the states are revisited during revision or as part of probability calculation.

B gRPC and Microservices in Healthcare

Several open-source high-performance RPC communication frameworks for microservice architectures have emerged over the years, Google gRPC (Humphries et al., 2018; Indrasiri and Kuruppu, 2020),[10] Apache Thrift (Rakowski, 2015; Abernethy, 2019),[11] and Finagle from Twitter (Eriksen, 2014),[12] among several others. Our work adopts gRPC not least because of its feature maturity, stability, popularity in the industry and academia, as well as the availability of security mechanisms, crucial in microservice environments (Yarygina, 2018; Pereira-Vale et al., 2021), which it provides out of the box.

There is a growing body of literature either solely devoted to or mentioning the use of microservices architectures in healthcare, in particular in health information systems (HIS) (Mavrogiorgou et al., 2021), mobility (Melis et al., 2016; Rendulich et al., 2019; Mukhiddinov and Cho, 2021), physiotherapy (Caporuscio et al., 2017; Postolache et al., 2019), and elderly patients care (Dobre et al., 2021; Panchea et al., 2021). Furthermore, there is a growing awareness of the importance of flexible software architectures in assistive technologies as the Web becomes even more ubiquitous (Yesilada and Harper, 2019). Our work investigates one such architecture in the area of text entry for AAC.

[10]https://grpc.io/

[11]https://thrift.apache.org/

[12]https://twitter.github.io/finagle/

```
// Model hub section.
model_hub_config {
  mixture_type: LINEAR_INTERPOLATION
  model_config {  // First model.
    type: PPM
    weight: 0.301  // -std::log10(0.5)
    storage {
      model_file: "${PRIVATE_TEXT_FILE}"
      ppm_options {
        max_order: 5  // 5-gram.
        static_model: false  // Dynamic.
      }
    }
  }
  model_config {  // Second model.
    type: CHAR_NGRAM_FST
    weight: 0.301  // -std::log10(0.5)
    storage {
      model_file: "${FST_FILE}"
      vocabulary_file: "${VOCAB_FILE}"
    }
  }
}
// Networking and authentication.
address_uri: "x.x.x.x:${PORT}"
auth {  // Authentication.
  tls {  // Transport layer security.
    // Strings below are PEM-encoded.
    private_key: "..."
    // Public certificate.
    server_cert: "..."
    // Custom certificate authority.
    custom_ca_cert: "..."
    // Require valid client certificate.
    client_verify: true
  }
}
```

Table 1: Example microservice configuration consisting of two linearly interpolated dynamic and static models.

C Practical Example

C.1 Configuration Language

We use the flexible text format of Google protocol buffers[13] as a configuration language for customizing the LM hub, where a number of different LM algorithms, their particular run-time parameters, types of tokens (e.g., character or word-based models), alphabets, and various prediction blending techniques can be defined for a particular LM hub configuration. Here we present a concrete example of this configuration language.

Table 1 shows an example of a two-model configuration using this syntax that may correspond to the model hub running locally (Figure 3) or remotely (model hub H_A in Figure 4).

The configuration consists of two main sections: the LM hub, and the microservice settings for networking and authentication mechanisms. In this

[13]https://developers.google.com/protocol-buffers

particular configuration, the LM hub is configured to serve the linearly interpolated predictions from two models: the dynamic PPM 5-gram model (the first model in hub's configuration) and the character n-gram model encoded as a finite state transducer (FST) with unspecified model order (which is assumed to be stored in the model file) and explicitly specified external vocabulary file. Both models are contributing equally to the final prediction with interpolation weight $\lambda = 0.5$.[14] Also note, that in this example the dynamic model relies on the external text file (provided by the `PRIVATE_TEXT_FILE` environment variable) for initialization: this file is used to bootstrap the dynamic PPM model from user's previous typing history during the initialization, similar to implementation in Dasher. If the PPM file is empty or not provided, the model starts with a uniform distribution.

The second configuration section in our example contains the networking and authentication setup for the LM hub microservice: the IP address and the port of the network interface, as well as the configuration for the TLS authentication mechanism with the necessary cryptographic keys and certificates encoded as strings in Privacy Enhanced Mail (PEM) format (Josefsson and Leonard, 2015). Note that in this example the microservice authenticates all the client connections for added security by requiring the clients to present the valid client certificates, achieved by enabling the `client_verify` configuration flag.

C.2 Life of an Estimate

The simplified class diagram providing the details of the core LM hub components (excluding the gRPC-based microservice details) in Unified Modeling Language (UML) notation (Miles and Hamilton, 2006) is shown in Figure 6. The bare bones LM interface is provided by the `LanguageModel` abstract class from which the concrete implementations for the dynamic (`PpmModel`) and static (`CharNGramFstModel`) models discussed in the previous Section C.1 are derived. Each of the models implements its own input-output (I/O) mechanism and provides its own character inference engine. Each concrete model implements several prediction interfaces, such as obtaining probability distribution over the entire alphabet (`GetScores`) given the context (represented by

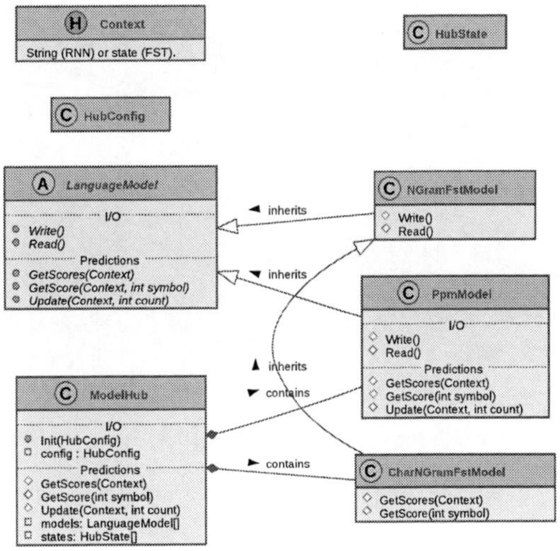

Figure 6: Simplified UML class diagram corresponding to the LM stack of configuration shown in Table 1.

the handle `Context` in the figure),[15] as well as querying for probabilities of individual symbols (`GetScore`). In addition, the dynamic model also provides a concrete implementation of dynamic updates of symbol counts (`Update`). Note that the character n-gram FST model derives from an intermediate abstract class shared by all the n-gram FST implementations (`NGramFstModel`). This class provides common functionality for representing n-grams within the FST formalism and is extended by other classes that implement character inference from more complex models, such as word-based n-grams (not shown in the figure).

The LM API that is integrated with the gRPC microservice layer is provided by the `ModelHub` class. It provides a facade over all the model and interpolation types provided by the configuration (`HubConfig`). The responsibility of this class is to manufacture the required LMs and provide a unified prediction and model update mechanism at run-time. Internally, the class maintains model and input-specific state (denoted `HubState` in the figure) for efficiency at inference time.

A simplified UML sequence diagram describing the sequence of events involved in establishing a gRPC connection with the remote LM hub (`Connect`) and performing a single inference query (`RPC GetScores`) is shown in Figure 7. In our

[14] Internally we represent the probabilities as negative log-likelihoods, hence the weights for both models in the configuration are set to be approximately equal to −0.301.

[15] The handle `Context` representing the current context in which the predictions or updates are to be made is implementation specific: for finite-state models, such as n-grams, this is simply an integer FST state ID. For neural models, this handle can point to a particular input string in a cache of histories.

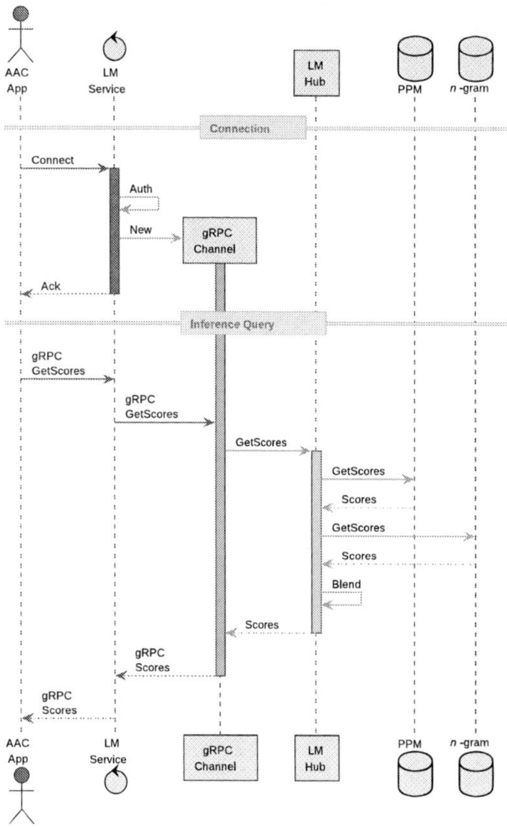

Figure 7: Simplified UML sequence diagram detailing the processing of a single inference query against the remote LM hub configured according to Table 1.

example the LM hub runs as a standalone gRPC microservice on a remote node. The network API (denoted `LM Service` in the figure) implements the RPC protocol that exposes the underlying LM hub API via portable gRPC protocol buffer messages for requests (such as `RPC GetScores`) and responses (`RPC Scores`). After authenticating the client and establishing a communication channel (denoted `gRPC Channel`) an asynchronous event loop within the service processes the incoming requests, dispatching them to LM hub engine for processing. In our example, the inference call `GetScores` to LM hub yields the predictions `Scores` blended from predictions of two models (PPM and n-gram). A gRPC response (`RPC Scores`) is then formed by the microservice and returned to the client application.

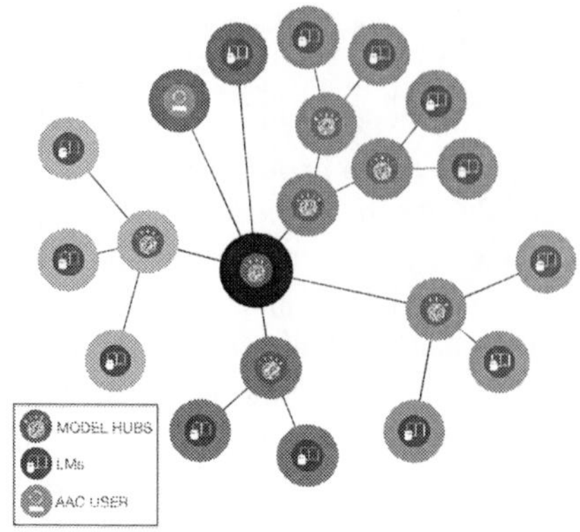

Figure 8: Hypothetical (and impractical) LM inference network over many models. The inference engines are not shown for brevity — the LM hubs directly use the models.

D Complex LM Hub Network Example

Allowing each LM hub microservice to both serve the models as well as securely communicate to other LM hub microservices allows one to construct significantly more complex inference architectures than the ones described above. One such hypothetical configuration is shown in Figure 8. In this example, the user interacts with a local hub (shown in a black node) that serves one local dynamic model (shown in a purple node). The local hub mixes the predictions from this dynamic model with the multiple predictions arriving via a complex network of other model hubs. The groups of nodes (hubs) and leafs (models) with the same color may denote the external organization providing the model service and hosting, specific types of models[16] or the provenance of the data the models were trained on (e.g., the medical domain). Needless to say, the LM microservices architectures of such complexity are unlikely to be required in practice, yet constructing configurations along the lines of the one shown in Figure 8 is definitely a feasible task in our framework.

[16] Such as XLNet (Yang et al., 2019), character-based BERT (El Boukkouri et al., 2020) and simpler transformer architectures (Al-Rfou et al., 2019).

ColorCode: A Bayesian Approach to Augmentative and Alternative Communication with Two Buttons

Matthew Daly
mattyrdaly@gmail.com

Abstract

Many people with severely limited muscle control can only communicate through augmentative and alternative communication (AAC) systems with a small number of buttons. In this paper, we present the design for ColorCode, which is an AAC system with two buttons that uses Bayesian inference to determine what the user wishes to communicate. Our information-theoretic analysis of ColorCode simulations shows that it is efficient in extracting information from the user, even in the presence of errors, achieving nearly optimal error correction. ColorCode is provided as open source software (https://github.com/mrdaly/ColorCode).

1 Introduction

People with limited muscle control, such as those affected by amyotrophic lateral sclerosis (ALS), can have trouble communicating through conventional means. Augmentative and alternative communication (AAC) systems can help these people communicate effectively (Glennen and DeCoste, 1997). These AAC systems can range from low-tech solutions, such as pointing to messages on a piece of paper (Scott, 1998), to high-tech solutions, such as eye-tracking software that allows someone to select keys on a keyboard with their gaze (Ball et al., 2010). The more limited the muscle control, the less information that can be input into an AAC system.

In this paper, we refer to any discrete input into an AAC system as a *button*, and a signal sent through a button as a *click*. Clicking a button (sometimes referred to as a *switch* in AAC contexts) can take many forms, such as twitching a particular muscle or looking to the left or right. People in the late stages of ALS may only be able to reliably click two different buttons. AAC systems for people with such limited muscle control must efficiently extract information from a small number of buttons to allow them to communicate effectively.

An effective AAC system for users with severely limited muscle control needs to be designed to allow the individual to use a small number of buttons to choose from a large number of options (like letters on a keyboard). A successful design must achieve this objective while also being easy to use and resilient to errors in the user's input. Designing a system that satisfies these properties is challenging.

There are many AAC software systems for a small number of buttons (e.g. Grid 3[1] and ACAT[2]). Most systems for two buttons involve a scanning keyboard where one button is used to scan through keys and the other button is used to select the chosen key (Colven and Judge, 2006). This method benefits from a simple interface, but it can take many clicks and therefore a lot of effort to communicate.

Previous research has used probabilistic reasoning and information-theoretic approaches to design effective AAC systems for few buttons (Ward et al., 2000; Broderick and MacKay, 2009; Higger et al., 2017). Common themes in this research include leveraging statistical language models to improve text entry and using concepts from information theory to analyze performance. In this work, we describe a new system whose design builds upon these existing ideas.

We present a new AAC system, named ColorCode, which allows users to communicate efficiently with only two buttons. ColorCode's interface is a virtual keyboard with characters the user can select to write sentences and communicate (see Figure 1a). Each key on the keyboard is assigned one of two colors, red or blue, and each of the two buttons is associated with one of the colors.

[1]Grid 3 is developed by Smartbox Assistive Technology Ltd.: https://thinksmartbox.com/product/grid-3/

[2]Assistive Context-Aware Toolkit (ACAT) is provided by Intel's Open Source Technology Center: https://01.org/acat/

Ninth Workshop on Speech and Language Processing for Assistive Technologies (SLPAT-2022), pages 17 - 23

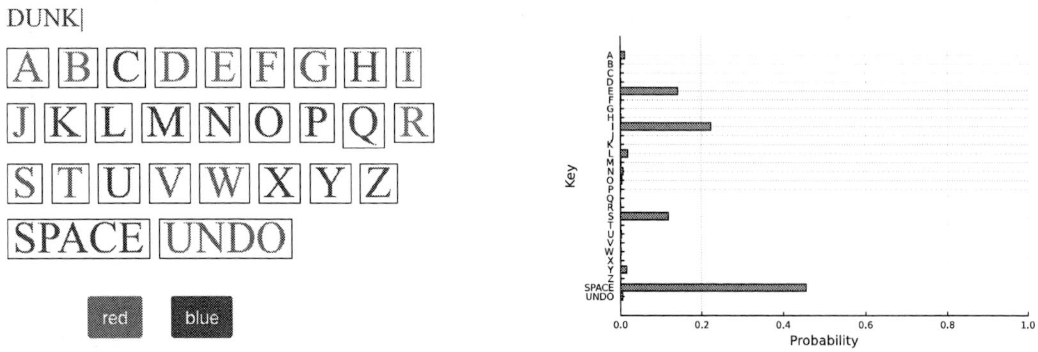

(a) ColorCode interface

(b) Belief over user's selection

Figure 1: ColorCode system after user has begun typing.

ColorCode repeatedly assigns colors to keys while observing the colors of the buttons the user clicks. The system uses Bayesian inference to update its belief over the user's chosen key given its observations of button clicks. An accurate language model and the intelligent assignment of colors to keys allow ColorCode to efficiently infer what the user wishes to type. Additionally, ColorCode adaptively corrects for errors in the user's input.

We simulate ColorCode on AAC-like text and record the average clicks per character. We analyze the results from an information-theoretic perspective to show that ColorCode efficiently extracts information from the user. We also simulate the input to ColorCode as a binary symmetric channel to empirically show that it is close to optimally resilient to errors in the user's input.

2 Related Work

This section gives a brief overview of previous research that used probabilistic reasoning and information-theoretic approaches to build AAC software systems for a small number of buttons.

2.1 Dasher

Dasher (Ward et al., 2000) uses the concept of arithmetic coding to allow users to efficiently type out messages. Although the original version of Dasher requires a continuous input method like controlling a mouse pointer or joystick, other extensions allow Dasher to be controlled by a small number of discrete buttons (MacKay et al., 2004).

2.2 Nomon

AAC systems for individuals who can only click one button use the timing of the click to convey information. Nomon (Broderick and MacKay, 2009) uses this type of input. For each option in Nomon's interface, there is a clock with a rotating hand. To select the option they want, the user clicks their button when the hand on the option's clock passes its noon marker. Nomon infers the user's choice (using Baye's rule) from the timings of the their clicks, and it adaptively learns the probability distribution of the user's click timings. The innovative design used by Nomon is very powerful and inspired much of the design of ColorCode. However, even though Nomon is resilient to timing errors in the user's clicks, some AAC users are not able to reliably time their clicks and therefore cannot use this input method. One of ColorCode's goals is to present a system that is as powerful as Nomon, but does not require the user to time their input.

2.3 Shuffle Speller

ColorCode is similar in several ways to Shuffle Speller (Higger et al., 2017), which is an AAC system designed for a brain-computer interface (BCI). Shuffle Speller assigns letters to different colors associated with buttons, and the user clicks buttons to choose a color. The users' brain signals are interpreted through the BCI as button clicks. Shuffle Speller uses Bayesian inference from the observed colors, and it chooses assignments of letters to colors to maximize the information it learns from observing a color. One key difference in Shuffle Speller's design is that it accounts for asymmetry in errors across the user's inputs. This additional complexity in modeling of input errors has the potential to improve the system's error correction.

We believe ColorCode's design is an improvement over Shuffle Speller in several ways. First, at each color assignment, Shuffle Speller moves the letters around the screen to fixed locations in the interface associated with the colors. In ColorCode, the letters are kept in static locations in a virtual keyboard while their colors change. This is designed to be more user friendly, since previous research suggests dynamic keyboard layouts increase the user's cognitive load and lead to slower text entry (Lesher et al., 1998; Johansen et al., 2003; Pouplin et al., 2014). Second, ColorCode uses adaptive "on-the-go" learning of the user's error rate as they use the system, but Shuffle Speller requires a calibration phase for the system to learn the distribution of the user's errors. Finally, Shuffle Speller uses a fixed prior probability for a "backspace", while ColorCode incorporates evidence from the user's previous input to form a more informed prior for the "undo" key (see Section 3.3), which is equivalent to Shuffle Speller's backspace.

3 Method

To type a message in ColorCode, the user first identifies the color of the key they wish to select (e.g. the letter A) and clicks the button for that color. After the user clicks a button, the system reassigns colors to all of the keys on the keyboard. The user repeats this process until the system selects the key they wanted and types the corresponding character in the display (or deletes a character if key was "undo"). ColorCode also plays an audible "click" sound to notify the user when a key is selected. See Figure 2 for a diagram demonstrating this process.

ColorCode maintains a belief over the user's desired key and uses Baye's rule to update its belief after observing the user's button click. The belief is a probability distribution over the possible keys (see Figure 1b). When the probability of a particular key reaches a certain threshold, the system selects that key. This probability threshold is set to 0.95 in ColorCode. If $P(k)$ is the probability the user wishes to select key k, and c is the color of the button the user clicks, we can compute the belief update using Baye's rule with:

$$P(k \mid c) = \frac{P(c \mid k)P(k)}{\sum_{k'} P(c \mid k')P(k')}$$

In this update, the two key components are the probability distributions $P(k)$ and $P(c \mid k)$, which are known as the *prior* and the *likelihood*, respectively.

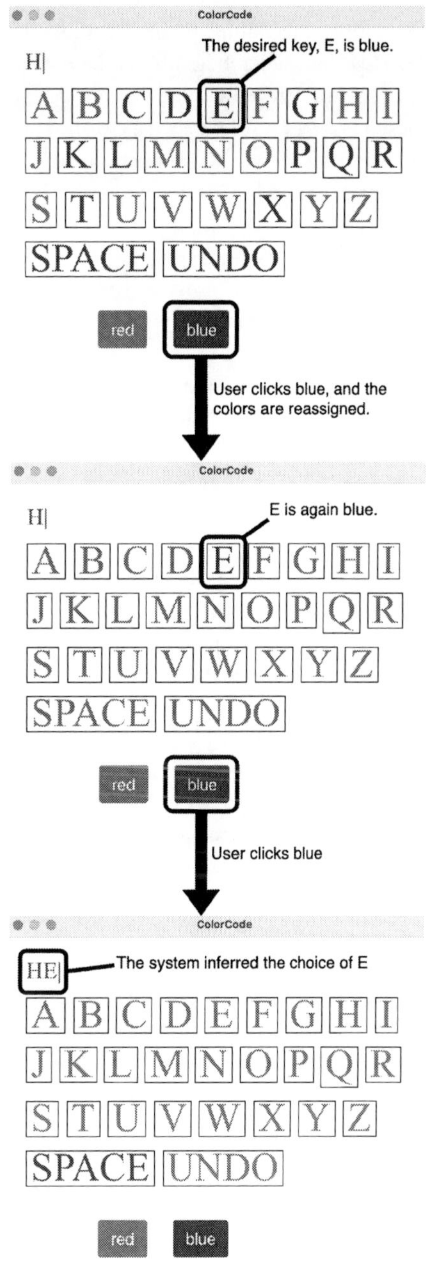

Figure 2: Diagram demonstrating process of selecting the letter E in ColorCode.

3.1 Prior

The prior is a probability distribution representing the previous belief over the user's key selection before the user clicks a button. When the user has already started clicking buttons to select a key, the prior is simply the output of the previous belief update. However, when beginning a key selection with no previous button clicks, we can define the prior based on any knowledge we have about which key the user will select. If we had no prior knowledge, the prior would be a uniform distribution over all the possible keys.

ColorCode uses a language model that uses the context of what the user previously typed to estimate the probability distribution over which character comes next. The 12-gram character language model[3] used by ColorCode was trained on billions of words of AAC-like text, providing a well-informed prior that allows ColorCode to infer the user's key selection in a few button clicks.

3.2 Likelihood

The likelihood, $P(c \mid k)$, is the probability that ColorCode would observe the color c from the user's click, given that they want to select the key k. If ColorCode always observed the user click the correct color button for the key they wished to select, then $P(c \mid k)$ would be 1 if c was the color of key k and 0 otherwise. However, it is possible that the user could make a mistake or the button's sensor could be noisy, and the system could observe a click for the wrong color. To account for these possible errors, we define the likelihood as the probability that the system observes the user click the correct color given their desired key and its color.

The system does not know the probability of a click error, so it must estimate it in some way. We assume the distribution of click errors is a stationary binary distribution with the parameter θ, which is the probability that the click is correct. ColorCode uses Bayesian learning to learn θ from observing correct and incorrect clicks from the user. Since the beta distribution is the conjugate prior of the binary distribution, we have:

$$P(\theta) = \text{Beta}(\theta \mid \alpha, \beta)$$

where α and β are parameters of the beta distribution. Each time the system observes the user correctly clicking a color button given their key, it increments α by 1, and it increments β when it observes the user clicking the incorrect button.

The parameters α and β can both be initialized to 1 to represent a uniform distribution over θ, but ColorCode starts with pseudocounts of $\alpha = 9$ and $\beta = 1$ to encode the belief that the probability of click errors is low. When computing the belief update, ColorCode uses the mean of the beta distribution:

$$P(c \mid k) = \begin{cases} \frac{\alpha}{\alpha+\beta} & \text{if } c \text{ is the color of } k \\ \frac{\beta}{\alpha+\beta} & \text{if } c \text{ is not the color of } k \end{cases}$$

It is not obvious how we can count when a user's click is correct or incorrect. ColorCode obtains these counts by keeping track of the user's clicks and the color assignments to keys, and then once a key is selected, it goes back and updates α and β assuming the selected key was the correct one.

When this likelihood is applied to the belief update, it corrects for the probability of error. If click errors are more likely, then the update increases (or decreases) the probability of keys by a smaller factor, therefore requiring more clicks to select a letter.

3.3 Undo

We include an "undo" key in ColorCode's interface to allow the user to indicate that the system incorrectly inferred the previous key selection. Many AAC systems have a similar option, often referred to as "backspace" or "delete". Many probabilistic AAC systems incorporate an undo key into the prior by fixing its probability to a predefined constant, such as 0.05, and then normalizing the rest of the keys' probabilities (e.g. Orhan et al., 2012; Higger et al., 2017). Fowler et al. (2013) introduces an algorithm that keeps track of probabilities for alternative inferences the system could have made, and then uses these probabilities to inform the prior probability of a backspace key.

In ColorCode, we set the undo probability to the probability that the previous key selection was wrong.[4] We know this probability from the belief the system had when it selected the previous key. When starting a new key selection, we have:

$$P(k_t = \text{UNDO}) = 1 - P(k_{t-1} = K)$$

where t is the current time step in terms of belief updates, and K is the key the system previously selected.

[3] https://imagineville.org/software/lm/dec19_char/

[4] During the first key selection, the undo probability is set to 0, since there are no key selections to undo.

When the user selects the undo key, the last character in the output string is removed. ColorCode then assumes that the selection of the removed character was incorrect, and the user still wishes to select the key that they originally intended to select. With this assumption, the system resets the prior to the belief it had at the time of the incorrect selection. However, it changes the probability of the assumed incorrect character to be the probability that the undo selection was wrong. After the system selected undo at step $t - 1$, we have:

$$P(k_t = K) = 1 - P(k_{t-1} = \text{UNDO})$$

where K is the key the system is assumed to have incorrectly selected before the undo. The probabilities of the rest of the keys are then normalized.

Additionally, when the user selects undo, ColorCode undoes the error rate learning it did on the previous key selection, since it can no longer assume that the selection was correct.

3.4 Color Assignment

An important aspect of ColorCode is the assignment of colors to keys at each step. This assignment determines what information the system learns when it observes a button click. In the degenerate case where all keys are assigned the same color, no information can be learned from a user's click. The goal of choosing a color assignment is to learn as much information as possible about the user's desired key selection.

We can use the entropy of observing a color as a heuristic to measure the effectiveness of a color assignment. The entropy, which can be thought of as the expected information content received from observing a user's color click, is defined as:

$$-\sum_{c} P(c) \log P(c)$$

where $P(c)$ is the probability of observing a click of color c based on our current belief.

Computing the entropy for every possible color assignment and choosing the maximum is intractable, but we can also maximize entropy by maximizing the uniformity of the probability distribution, $P(c)$ (MacKay, 2002). Choosing a color assignment that makes $P(c)$ as close to equiprobable as possible is equivalent to the partition problem, which is NP-complete. However, there are approximate algorithms for the partition problem that run in polynomial time, and ColorCode uses the simple greedy heuristic to approximate a solution (Korf, 1995).

We also tried assigning colors using Huffman coding, similar to Roark et al. (2013). While our simulations showed the Huffman coding approach performed slightly better than the partition approach with no click error, the partition approach performed better in the presence of errors. For this reason, ColorCode uses the partition approach for color assignments. A possible alternative would be to use Huffman coding when the system estimates an error rate below a certain threshold, and then use the partition approach if the error rate is above that threshold.

4 Results and Analysis

The effectiveness of ColorCode can be measured by the average number of clicks it takes the user to select a character. Low clicks per character (cpc) indicate that a system is efficient in its ability to extract information from the user.

Another important metric used to evaluate AAC systems is the text entry rate (TER). Measuring the text entry rate of a system requires a user study, which has not yet been performed using ColorCode (see Section 6).

We simulated ColorCode on a test set of AAC-like text, presented in Vertanen and Kristensson (2011), to calculate the average cpc. The simulator uses the undo key to correct any incorrect key selections, and these extra clicks are counted toward the cpc. Through these simulations, ColorCode achieved an average of 2.07 cpc.

We can analyze this result from an information-theoretic perspective by considering the theoretical lower bound on cpc given the language model ColorCode uses. We can view the color clicks as binary symbols (bits) in a variable-length encoding of the characters the user wishes to type. The source coding theorem for symbol codes states that the entropy of a character distribution is the lower bound on the expected number of bits required to encode a character (MacKay, 2002). However, the system uses a language model for the encoding because it does not know the true character distribution. So instead, the cross-entropy between the true distribution and the model distribution can be used as a lower bound on the expected number of bits per character in a coding scheme that uses the model distribution to encode characters that come from the true distribution (Brown et al., 1992). The cross-entropy is defined as:

$$-\mathbb{E}_{x \sim P(x)}[\log M(x \mid x_{-1}, x_{-2}, \dots)]$$

where $P(x)$ is the true distribution of characters and $M(x \mid x_{-1}, x_{-2}, \dots)$ is the language model's probability of a character given its context. To calculate the cross-entropy empirically, we estimate the expectation over the true distribution by averaging over the AAC test set used to evaluate ColorCode. Using this approach with the language model that ColorCode uses, we calculate the cross-entropy to be 1.73 bits. This means that ColorCode achieves 2.07 cpc when the lower bound given its language model is 1.73 cpc.

4.1 Error Correction

To evaluate ColorCode's resilience to click errors, we ran simulations on the test set with a parameter f, which defined the probability that the simulator would randomly click the incorrect color for the desired key.

Let us consider the user's clicks as bits being communicated over a noisy channel, specifically a binary symmetric channel (BSC). The BSC has a probability f of a bit flip (the color is incorrect) and a probability of $1 - f$ of a correct bit transmission (the color is correct). Error-correcting codes can be used to communicate over noisy channels by sending more bits for redundancy. Recall that ColorCode learns the click error rate and then requires more clicks from the user to compensate for more errors. Let us think of this mechanism in ColorCode as an error-correcting code.

We can evaluate an error-correcting code by its *information rate*, which is the ratio of information bits communicated to the total number of bits sent over the channel. The total number of bits includes both the information bits and the redundant bits which are sent to correct any errors. We can measure the information rate of ColorCode by using simulations on the test set. We define the number of information bits as the number of clicks required during a simulation with no error rate. Then we define the total number of bits as the total number of clicks the simulation requires when given an error rate f. With this, we can calculate the information rate of ColorCode for a given error rate.

According to the noisy-channel coding theorem, the error rate of a noisy channel can be corrected to an arbitrarily small resulting error (MacKay, 2002). Additionally, any error-correcting code that can achieve this has a maximum information rate equal to the *channel capacity*, C, of the channel. The channel capacity of a BSC with error rate f is

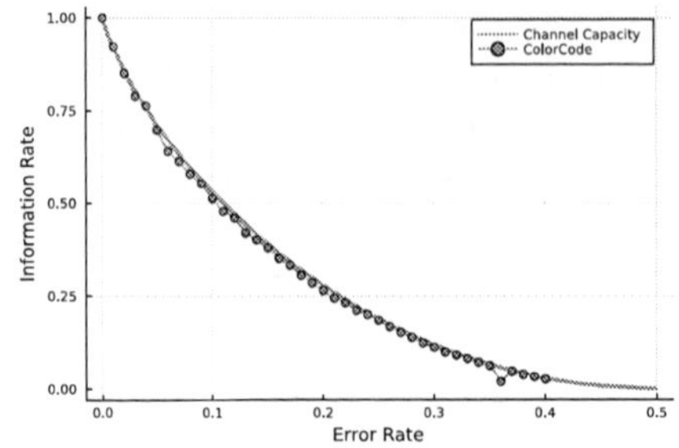

Figure 3: Plot comparing the information rate of ColorCode to the channel capacity of a binary symmetric channel.

$$C = 1 - h_2(f)$$

where h_2 is the binary entropy function.

We plot the information rates from our simulations in Figure 3, along with the optimal information rates of a BSC, the channel capacity. These empirical results show that ColorCode's error correction is nearly optimal when we model the errors with a BSC.

5 Conclusions

This paper presents the design of ColorCode, a new and powerful AAC system for two buttons. ColorCode combines a powerful language model, Bayesian learning of click errors, an informed undo operation, and intelligent color assignments into a Bayesian belief framework that uses a simple interface to efficiently extract information from the user. Our results demonstrate this efficiency by showing ColorCode requires an average of only 2.07 clicks to select a character, which is within one half of a click of the theoretical lower bound which is 1.73 clicks. ColorCode remains efficient in extracting information when there are errors in the input, and our results show that ColorCode handles errors with nearly optimal efficiency. These results show that ColorCode's design has the potential to help people who cannot communicate easily.

6 Future Work

Further development on ColorCode can make it viable for real-world use as an AAC system. Several improvements to the design could increase performance by making it easier for users to convey information. One improvement would be to extend ColorCode to optionally use more than two colors, which would help if the user has more control and can click more than two buttons. We could also improve the design with word predictions or other possible methods that would leverage the powerful language model to let the user select multiple characters with one click.

Additionally, conducting a user study with ColorCode is a vital next step in its development. Testing ColorCode with real users and real input devices is essential to evaluating its text entry rate, interface usability, and error correction.

Acknowledgements

Special thanks to Mykel Kochenderfer and Keith Vertanen.

References

Laura J Ball, Amy S Nordness, Susan K Fager, Katie Kersch, Brianae Mohr, Gary L Pattee, and David R Beukelman. 2010. Eye-gaze access to AAC technology for people with amyotrophic lateral sclerosis. *Journal of Medical Speech-Language Pathology*, 18(3):11.

Tamara Broderick and David J. C. MacKay. 2009. Fast and flexible selection with a single switch. *PLOS ONE*, 4(10):1–8.

Peter F Brown, Stephen A Della Pietra, Vincent J Della Pietra, Jennifer C Lai, and Robert L Mercer. 1992. An estimate of an upper bound for the entropy of english. *Computational Linguistics*, 18(1):31–40.

David Colven and Simon Judge. 2006. Switch access to technology. *ACE Centre Advisory Trust*.

Andrew Fowler, Brian Roark, Umut Orhan, Deniz Erdogmus, and Melanie Fried-Oken. 2013. Improved inference and autotyping in EEG-based BCI typing systems. In *International ACM SIGACCESS Conference on Computers and Accessibility*, New York, NY, USA. Association for Computing Machinery.

Sharon L Glennen and DC DeCoste. 1997. Augmentative and alternative communication systems. *The Handbook of Augmentative and Alternative Communication*, pages 59–69.

Matt Higger, Fernando Quivira, Murat Akcakaya, Mohammad Moghadamfalahi, Hooman Nezamfar, Mujdat Cetin, and Deniz Erdogmus. 2017. Recursive Bayesian coding for BCIs. *IEEE Transactions on Neural Systems and Rehabilitation Engineering*, 25(6):704–714.

Anders S Johansen, John P Hansen, Dan W Hansen, Kenji Itoh, and Satoru Mashino. 2003. Language technology in a predictive, restricted on-screen keyboard with dynamic layout for severely disabled people. In *EACL Workshop on Language Modeling for Text Entry Methods*.

Richard E. Korf. 1995. From approximate to optimal solutions: A case study of number partitioning. In *International Joint Conference on Artificial Intelligence*, page 266–272.

Gregory Lesher, Bryan Moulton, and D Jeffery Higginbotham. 1998. Techniques for augmenting scanning communication. *Augmentative and Alternative Communication*, 14(2):81–101.

David J. C. MacKay. 2002. *Information Theory, Inference & Learning Algorithms*. Cambridge University Press.

David JC MacKay, Chris J Ball, and Mick Donegan. 2004. Efficient communication with one or two buttons. In *AIP Conference Proceedings*, volume 735, pages 207–218. American Institute of Physics.

Umut Orhan, Kenneth E. Hild, Deniz Erdogmus, Brian Roark, Barry Oken, and Melanie Fried-Oken. 2012. RSVP keyboard: An EEG based typing interface. In *2012 IEEE International Conference on Acoustics, Speech and Signal Processing (ICASSP)*, pages 645–648.

Samuel Pouplin, Johanna Robertson, Jean-Yves Antoine, Antoine Blanchet, Jean-Loup Kahloun, Philippe Volle, Justine Bouteille, Frédéric Lofaso, and Djamel Bensmail. 2014. Effect of a Dynamic Keyboard and Word Prediction Systems on Text Input Speed in Patients with Functional Tetraplegia. *Journal of Rehabilitation Research and Development*, 51(3):467–480.

Brian Roark, Russell Beckley, Chris Gibbons, and Melanie Fried-Oken. 2013. Huffman scanning: Using language models within fixed-grid keyboard emulation. *Computer Speech & Language*, 27(6):1212–1234.

Janet Scott. 1998. Low tech methods of augmentative communication. *Augmentative Communication in Practice 2*.

Keith Vertanen and Per Ola Kristensson. 2011. The imagination of crowds: Conversational AAC language modeling using crowdsourcing and large data sources. In *Conference on Empirical Methods in Natural Language Processing (EMNLP)*, pages 700–711. ACL.

David J. Ward, Alan F. Blackwell, and David J. C. MacKay. 2000. Dasher—a data entry interface using continuous gestures and language models. In *ACM Symposium on User Interface Software and Technology*, page 129–137.

A glimpse of assistive technology in daily life

Preethi Vaidyanathan, Augustine Webster, Amy Diego,
Doug Sawyer, Angela Wilson, Jenn Rubenstein, Katerina Fassov, James Brinton
Eyegaze, Inc., Fairfax, Virginia, USA
preethi@eyegaze.com, kathykwebster@gmail.com, amydiego@gmail.com
dsawyer1007@gmail.com, ajbwheels@gmail.com, jenn.rubenstein@eyegaze.com
katerina@eyegaze.com, james.brinton@eyegaze.com

Abstract

Robitaille (2010) wrote 'if all technology companies have accessibility in their mind then people with disabilities won't be left behind.' Current technology has come a long way from where it stood decades ago; however, researchers and manufacturers often do not include people with disabilities in the design process and tend to accommodate them after the fact. In this paper we share feedback from four assistive technology users who rely on one or more assistive technology devices in their everyday lives. We believe end users should be part of the design process and that by bringing together experts and users, we can bridge the research/practice gap.

1 Introduction

"i am hungry." types 21-year-old Augie on his augmentative and alternative communication (AAC) device. Augie is one of many people who uses a switch to access a communication device. Similar to the switch, there are several other assistive technology (AT) devices that can be deemed as capability enhancers ranging from reading glasses to brain-computer interfaces (Robitaille, 2010). These devices help an individual overcome some of the limitations due to their disability and continue major life activities.

Despite the advances in the technology, factors such as affordability, access, learning curve, usability and pandemics (e.g. COVID-19) can limit who gets to use these AT devices (Madara Marasinghe, 2016; Alabbas and Miller, 2019; Rasouli et al., 2021; Naghavi et al., 2022). We believe involving the users early on in the process of design will help us bridge the gap sooner and better (Shah and Robinson, 2007; van de Kar and Den Hengst, 2009). Largely, researchers and manufacturers tend to obtain a generic survey of features from a pool of users or involve few users to some depth in the design process. Many of these approaches lack in-depth diverse involvement of users. Additionally, due to various reasons the information obtained remains within the reaches of the group that is central to the collection. We need an open platform approach to bring together users, scientists, and manufacturers.

Many existing platforms are scientifically oriented, and we observed that users may not necessarily have scientific evidence to hypotheses to actively participate. Therefore, their involvement gets limited to an attendee or spectator or panel member. The goal of this paper is to provide users an opportunity to get involved and actively participate by sharing how some of these AT devices have empowered them. We also share some of the unmet challenges that exist in the current technologies.

We crafted seven questions that were answered by four users (also co-authors) via email using their respective devices. These simple questions were formulated by a product engineer and a speech-language pathologist who have worked for approximately 5 years with various users of AT, and were designed to elicit responses that would highlight the user experience to the forefront of researchers' minds. The questions range from asking users about their experience obtaining their AT device (since many devices are not easy and quick to obtain due to their funding process) to how easy or difficult it is to use it (many devices have a complex learning curve.

In the next sections we share the feedback from each user word for word as typed using their respective devices. Therefore, there may exist typographical and formatting errors. Please note, this paper does not intend to analyze any AAC device or a company's product.

2 Amy Diego

1. **What assistive technology (hardware or software; low-tech or high-tech) do you**

Ninth Workshop on Speech and Language Processing for Assistive Technologies (SLPAT-2022), pages 24 - 29
May 27, 2022 ©2022 Association for Computational Linguistics

use? I use an Eye gaze Edge communication device.

2. **How difficult was it to find the solution or device you use?** It was not difficult to obtain. We got the referral from UCSF .

3. **How difficult is it to use your solution or device?** My eye gaze device wasn't hard to use initially. We have a great person who helped us get up and running and we have her to touch base with if I have problems . Also, on the device there are videos for all kinds of trouble shooting problems.

4. **What are two important problems that your device or solution solves?** ALS is a debilitating disease that has robbed my ability to move and speak . The Eye gaze Edge has solved problems of communication and entertainment . I can speak freely to my family that no alphabet board can do . I can get in touch with my friends and I love being able to communicate independently . Entertainment - wise, I can watch Netflix on it, shop on Amazon, connect on Facebook and Instagram, and use the web for anything.I love it!

5. **What are two important problems that your current solution or device does not solve?** Two problems that the Eye gaze doesn't solve are minor issues . When I am texting friends, I often need to say the same thing to many people . I can't do group texts . Also, I receive texts that have a link but I can't open the link.

6. **How do you think improvements could be made to one's Assistive Technology experience?** There isn't much that the eye gaze doesn't solve. The above mentioned issues would be worthwhile to look into. I'd love to see the pictures and links from texts without asking my husband. Overall, the device helps tremendously in keeping me independent and in touch with my family and friends.

7. **Tell us a little bit about your background (could be school, work, or interests or hobbies).** Having grown up with a dad who was a lifeguard Captain, I have always loved the beach. I miss watching my kids in the sand and my hubby running around with the dog. Love the sound of the waves and the taste of saltwater on my lips. I left the best job ever when I got my diagnosis .I was teaching K/1 at the same school with my kids. My daughter would have lunch in my classroom with her friends. I loved my "littles" and would be excited to go to work everyday. My other hobby that I miss are drum lessons. I've always loved music and there isn't a memory that I have that isn't connected by a some song. When I started playing drums, it was fun to try and learn these songs.

3 Augustine Webster

1. **What assistive technology (hardware or software; low-tech or high-tech) do you use?** I use a PRC Accent 1400 with two "bluetooth" freedom switches. One scans and one selects. The scanner is mounted to the left side of my head and the selector is at the back of my head. both are mounted on a whitmyer headrest. I also say yes by looking up and no by looking to the side.

2. **How difficult was it to find the solution or device you use?** I cannot use my fingers to type. it was challenging for therapists and my mom to figure it out. From age two to seven I had a dynavox with 4 boxes, but I couldn't hit it accurately with my hands. During that time my mom found different therapists who experimented with switches by my knees, elbows, and head. The Switch It games helped me get the scan/select system down. The PRC device worked well with 2 switches, the Dynovox did not. I have tried eye gaze without success ad the ablenet orange and white switch for the i pad but i cant remember the pattern.

3. **How difficult is it to use your solution or device?** It is easy for me to use my device, when it is charged and working, and when the batteries work in my switches. Some people say I play it like a piano. I know some patterns by heart. like "i am hungry." The switches use CR2032 lithium batteries 3 volt and last about 1 week. My switches wear out about every six months. I could use wire switches and I did for years, but my athetoid movements often disconnect the wires. And when I did use wire switches the internal ports wore out bc i often

yanked the switches out by accident due to my crazy body. I really like the wireless switches but it is expensive to replace them and their batteries.

4. **What are two important problems that your device or solution solves?** I can express my wants and needs, make jokes, and communicate.

5. **What are two important problems that your current solution or device does not solve?** I cannot access the internet at all. I cannot read long texts when texting. A very smart person has to pair my phone to my device and not all my aids or school team knows how to do that.

6. **How do you think improvements could be made to one's Assistive Technology experience?** I am going to see a new therapist Monday to see if I can manage a 1-switch system to surf the internet. I cannot email or surf You Tube, I have to ask everyone to help me. I want to be able to navigate an I Pad or computer all by myself to go where I want and email who I want and be on social media. I will have to look at a blue line that moves horizontally on the screen click when it gets to what I want and then follow a vertical blue line to stop where I want. then the device goes at the crosspoint. This kind of system has been hard for me but there is a new one so I am going to try it.

   My body moves too much so eye gaze doesn't work for me. also i have blue eyes and my retinas are pink and not always picked up be the infrared eye gaze systems.

   I would like 1 device that is my Accent and have it be an ipad and phone that I can control to communicate with the synthesized voice and surf the internet to watch cooking shows, do research on restaurants, and connect on the social media channels. I have 100s of pages that my mom and teachers have programmed over the past 14 years...it is like my library..i can't imagine not having access to it. But I think I might need 2 devices. my accent and an ipad mounted to my chair. I love youtube and probably wouldn't need an aid all day if I could navigate it on my own. I'd like to have some switches in my bed to play music when I wake up.

7. **Tell us a little bit about your background (could be school, work, or interests or hobbies).** I am 21 years old. I like to go out to eat, go to concerts, and visit with friends. I love to tell stories. I write them and then my mom programs them into my device so I don't have to type one word at a time. I have attended Fairfax County Public Schools since I was 2 years old and received a lot of help with assisitive technology. I am an assitive technology ambassador for FCPS and have shown many kids with mobility challenges how I navigate. One boy's mom found my mom on Facebook and thanked her for braving the world of "Augie"mentative communication. He was 6 when I showed him how and now he uses 2 switches and writes book reports. I like jokes and puns. I like to talk about NFL with my dad. I remember all the books my mom reads and remind her of them when she can't remember. I hope I can find a job in 2023 because that is when school ends for me. I would like to work at Jills House, a respite program for kids. I would choose the menus and movies and talk to the kids. My favorite TV show is Speechless. My favorite movie is Major Payne. My favorite restaurant is Social Burger in Vienna. My favorite band is Peter, Paul & Mary.

4 Angela Wilson

1. **What assistive technology (hardware or software; low-tech or high-tech) do you use?** Jaco Robotic Arm

2. **How difficult was it to find the solution or device you use?** It was easy I saw it on you tube and on Instagram and I asked my occupational therapist about it and she had the company fly out to my house and let me try the arm out.

3. **How difficult is it to use your solution or device?** There's definitely a learning curve. There are sixteen different directions and four different modes to learn. With time it gets easier to use.

4. **What are two important problems that your device or solution solves?** If I drop

something on the floor I can pick it up. I can also open doors and push elevator buttons without assistance from someone.

5. **What are two important problems that your current solution or device does not solve?** I can't use it for two handed things. I can't feed myself with it because I use a syringe so you need two hands for that. I also can't open jars and containers because again you need two hands.

6. **How do you think improvements could be made to one's Assistive Technology experience?** I think it would be better if the hand was more realistic. Also if it had five fingers. Instead of three. Also if would be cool is if came with something to hold objects in place while you used the arm to open the lid.

7. **Tell us a little bit about your background (could be school, work, or interests or hobbies).** I was born with a rare form of muscular dystrophy called Spinal Muscular Atrophy. It's similar to ALS, basically my muscles get weak over time. My life expectancy was the age of 3 and today I am 40 years young! Life is relatively normal for me and I use many devices throughout the day to help me do everyday tasks. I just recently decided to go back to school . I'm pursuing my masters degree in Criminal Justice. I'm obsessed with crime documentaries so I decided why not get a degree in something that I'm really interested. In my free time I enjoy volunteering at Muttville in San Francisco. They are a wonderful senior dog rescue. I also became a foster with them and I have successfully helped 3 dogs find their forever homes!

5 Doug Sawyer

1. **What assistive technology (hardware or software; low-tech or high-tech) do you use?** My high-tech solution is a system called EYEGAZE EDGE .It is a Tablet-based product that utilizes an IR-based camera to track eye movement. The software runs on Microsoft 10 OS.

   My low-tech standby solution is a simple letter board piece of paper with a matrix of letters.

2. **How difficult was it to find the solution or device you use?** My hunt to find a solution was not that difficult. Children's Hospital in Massachusetts has a department dedicated to helping individuals find the proper communication-assisted technology for their needs. During my visit to the hospital, I was able to try various products from different manufacturers to find the right solution for my application.

3. **How difficult is it to use your solution or device?** The device is straightforward once one master's eye control. The layout of the software models causes a little difficulty during online meetings, and the inability to engage three keyboard keys at once causes a problem.

4. **What are two important problems that your device or solution solves?** My device's first and most obvious solution is communication in general. This allows me to work and maintain some level of dignity and self-worth..

5. **What are two important problems that your current solution or device does not solve?** Because sunlight interferes with IR cameras, my device will not function in direct sunlight. Also, the camera on my device can get out of focus. Without assistance from another individual to adjust the camera, I am stuck without communication.

6. **How do you think improvements could be made to one's Assistive Technology experience?** Enable the user to go outside and enjoy the sunshine. Provide full functional private phone capability.

7. **Tell us a little bit about your background (could be school, work, or interests or hobbies).** I have an MSEE and MBA. Work full-time in new product development. I love the outdoors and watching all sports.

6 Discussion

The shared direct-from-user responses show that existing AT solutions have helped users perform some of the tasks they could not do otherwise, enjoy some of the activities they would have been deprived of, and above all given them back their autonomy and dignity. However, we also recognize that many of these solutions are comprised of multiple incompatible components, not providing an overall solution to their needs and in some cases quite difficult to use thereby limiting the usage.

Although there are many centers and clinics that offer ways to try out the devices, obtaining a device becomes little difficult due to the expertise involved in finding the right to solution for a given individual e.g., User 3, Augie had to consult with different therapists and needed some experiment before finding the right device. Additionally, many of these devices require at least some level of training for the care-givers or aids at home, school, or workplace. Likewise using these devices to do what an individual would do on their computer or phone has improved over the past few years but often the available features and usability is specific to the type of AT device or manufacturer. For example, User 1 Amy who uses an Eyegaze Edge can access internet without much issue whereas Augie currently cannot access internet at all. In most cases the respective devices need some kind of intervention by a caregiver or family member e.g., User 4 Doug's device would go out of focus and then he is stuck without communication until another individual provides assistance. The responses shared above certainly highlight the positive features of current AT devices and how they improve everyday lives. Some of these improvements are that users can now access internet, their phones and computers, smart home devices etc. using their AT devices. However, these improvements seem like afterthoughts. Accommodation for the disability population happens after the actual device or technology has been designed and become mainstream.

Participants experience a range of ease-of-use with AT products, ranging from "easy-to-use" and difficult or complex. All participants were able to identify features in their technology that improved their lives and allowed them to communicate or access communication platforms. Participants were also able to identify limits their AT devices had, with a majority of participants identifying real-life scenarios where their access to communication or participation were limited. Responses also identified challenges with AT not always being durable and long-lasting, expensive and requiring assistance from others to set up or maintain use over time. Each participant was able to suggest solutions to solve these problems. These themes highlight that AT users experience real challenges that spark ideas for possible solutions; also 100% of participants expressed current solutions made possible by the AT they use. From these interviews, we would suggest researchers look at asking similar questions to a larger sample size across a wider specrum of AT devices (communication, mobility, computer access) to ask and understand, "How can AT manufacturers collaborate with AT users to innovate functional design? What are ways to improve AT ease-of-use, durability, and increase access to communication in text and spoken forms?"

We acknowledge not all the issues presented in the user responses are directly related to Computational Linguistics or Natural Language Processing e.g., a robotic arm looking and feeling more realistic or an eye tracker that would work in the sunlight. However, we believe many of these challenges are multimodal e.g., existing AAC devices used via touch/headmouse/switch/gaze are used for communication with another human, with the computer or phone, with the internet. If we could bring AT users, NLP experts, Computer Vision scientists, clinicians, engineers, caregivers, policy-makers and others together we could bridge the research/practice gap sooner and more efficiently. The sample size we present here is small, but we find it significant that each participant was able to share the current limitations of their device and suggestions for improvements; this is where a 'a gap to be bridged' is illustrated by these interviews. We hope this paper is a step forward in bringing the users to the design table and work toward solutions that give them back their autonomy and dignity.

References

Norah Abdullah Alabbas and Darcy E Miller. 2019. Challenges and assistive technology during typical routines: Perspectives of caregivers of children with autism spectrum disorders and other disabilities. *International Journal of Disability, Development and Education*, 66(3):273–283.

Keshini Madara Marasinghe. 2016. Assistive technologies in reducing caregiver burden among informal caregivers of older adults: a systematic review. *Disability and Rehabilitation: Assistive Technology*, 11(5):353–360.

Azam Naghavi, Salar Faramarzi, Ali Abbasi, and

Samira-Sadat Badakhshiyan. 2022. Covid-19 and challenges of assistive technology use in iran. *Disability and Rehabilitation: Assistive Technology*, pages 1–7.

Omid Rasouli, Lisbeth Kvam, Vigdis Schnell Husby, Monica Røstad, and Aud Elisabeth Witsø. 2021. Understanding the possibilities and limitations of assistive technology in health and welfare services for people with intellectual disabilities, staff perspectives. *Disability and Rehabilitation: Assistive Technology*, pages 1–9.

Suzanne Robitaille. 2010. *The Illustrated Guide to Assistive Technology and Devices: Tools and Gadgets for Living Independently: Easyread Super Large 18pt Edition*. ReadHowYouWant. com.

Syed Ghulam Sarwar Shah and Ian Robinson. 2007. Benefits of and barriers to involving users in medical device technology development and evaluation. *International journal of technology assessment in health care*, 23(1):131–137.

Elisabeth van de Kar and Mariëlle Den Hengst. 2009. Involving users early on in the design process: closing the gap between mobile information services and their users. *Electronic Markets*, 19(1):31–42.

A comparison study on patient-psychologist voice diarization

Rachid Riad * and **Hadrien Titeux*** and **Xuan Nga Cao** and **Emmanuel Dupoux**
CoML, ENS/CNRS/EHESS/INRIA/PSL Research University

Laurie Lemoine and **Justine Montillot** and **Agnes Sliwinski**
and **Jennifer Hamet Bagnou** and **Anne-Catherine Bachoud-Lévi**
NPI, ENS/INSERM/UPEC/HD CENTER/PSL Research University

Abstract

Conversations between a clinician and a patient, in natural conditions, are valuable sources of information for medical follow-up. The automatic analysis of these dialogues could help extract new language markers and speed up the clinicians' reports. Yet, it is not clear which model is the most efficient to detect and identify the speaker turns, especially for individuals with speech disorders. Here, we proposed a split of the data that allows conducting a comparative evaluation of different diarization methods. We designed and trained end-to-end neural network architectures to directly tackle this task from the raw signal and evaluate each approach under the same metric. We also studied the effect of fine-tuning models to find the best performance. Experimental results are reported on naturalistic clinical conversations between Psychologists and Interviewees, at different stages of Huntington's disease, displaying a large panel of speech disorders. We found out that our best end-to-end model achieved 19.5% IER on the test set, compared to 23.6% achieved by the finetuning of the X-vector architecture. Finally, we observed that we could extract clinical markers directly from the automatic systems, highlighting the clinical relevance of our methods.

1 Introduction

During the last decades, it became easier to collect large naturalistic corpora of speech data. It is now possible to obtain new realistic measurements of turn-takings and linguistic behaviours (Ash and Grossman, 2015). These measurements can be especially useful during clinical interviews as they augment the current clinical panel of assessments and unlock home-based assessments (Matton et al., 2019). The remote automatic measure of symptoms of patients with Neurodegenerative diseases could greatly improve the follow-up of patients and speed-up ongoing clinical trials.

Yet, this methodology relies on the heavy burden of manual annotation to reach the necessary amount needed to draw significant conclusions. It is now indispensable to have robust speech processing pipelines to extract meaningful insights from these long naturalistic datasets (Lahiri et al., 2020). Huntington's Disease represents a unique opportunity to design and test these speech algorithms for *Neurodegenerative diseases*. Indeed, individuals with the Huntington's disease can exhibit a large spectrum of *speech and language* symptoms (Vogel et al., 2012) and it is possible to follow gene carriers even before the official clinical onset of the disease (Hinzen et al., 2018). The first unavoidable computational tasks to extract speech and linguistic information from medical interviews is the diarization: (1) the *detection* of speaker-homogeneous portions of voice activity (Graf et al., 2015) and (2) the *identification* of speaker (Bigot et al., 2010). Speaker turns are clinically informative for diagnostic in Huntington's Disease (Perez et al., 2018; Vogel et al., 2012).

First, a number of studies are trying to solve this problem directly from the audio signal and linguistic outputs, also referred to as *Speaker Role Recognition*. They are taking advantage of the specificities (ex: prosody, specific vocabulary, adapted language models) of each role in the different domains: Broadcast news programs (Bigot et al., 2010), Meetings (Sapru and Valente, 2012), Medical conversations (Flemotomos et al., 2018), Child-centered recordings (Lavechin et al., 2020;

* Equal contribution. We are very thankful to the patients that participated in our study. We thank Katia Youssov, Laurent Cleret de Langavant, Marvin Lavechin, and the speech pathologists for the multiple helpful discussions and the evaluations of the patients. This work is funded in part by the Agence Nationale pour la Recherche (ANR-17-EURE-0017 Frontcog, ANR-10-IDEX-0001-02 PSL*, ANR-19-P3IA-0001 PRAIRIE 3IA Institute) and Grants from Neuratris, from Facebook AI Research (Research Gift), Google (Faculty Research Award), Microsoft Research (Azure Credits and Grant), and Amazon Web Service (AWS Research Credits).

Ninth Workshop on Speech and Language Processing for Assistive Technologies (SLPAT-2022), pages 30 - 36

Figure 1: Two approaches for the diarization of conversational clinical interviews. The steps for the Speaker Enrollment Protocol are in Blue, and Green for the Speaker Role Recognition.

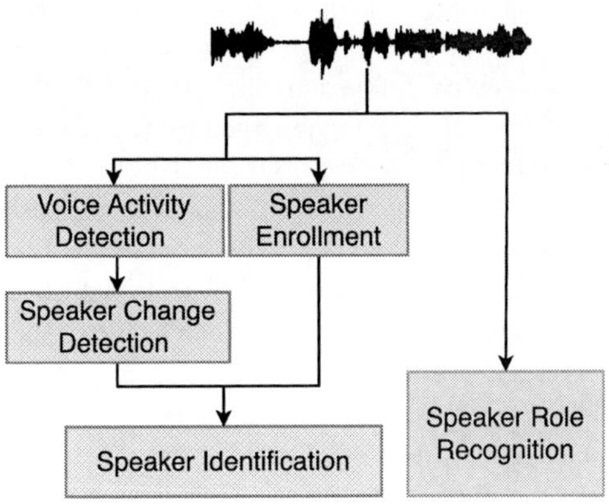

Koluguri et al., 2020).

Another approach relies on *Speaker Enrollment* (Snyder et al., 2017; Heigold et al., 2016), it aims to check the identity of a given speech segment based on a enrolled speaker template. Our study differ from these studies as they are evaluating their pipelines with already segmented speaker-homogeneous speech segments. Another related approach is *Personal VAD* (Voice Activity Detection) model from (Ding et al., 2020) where they used enrolled speaker template to detect speech segments from each individual speaker.

None of these approaches have been compared under the same evaluation metric, despite prior works aiming at solving both these tasks (García et al., 2019) and their high degree of similarities.

Here in this paper, we aimed to *detect* automatically the portions of speech and to *identify* the speakers in medical conversation between Psychologists and Interviewees. These interviewees are either Healthy Controls (C), gene carriers without overt manifestation of Huntington's Disease (preHD) and manifest gene carriers of Huntington's Disease (HD). We introduced a novel way to split the datasets so that we are now capable to compare two different speech processing approaches to deal with these 2 problems (Figure 1): *Speaker Role Recognition* and *Speaker Enrollment Protocol*. We showed the clinical relevance of these pipelines with the extraction speech markers that have been found predictive in Huntington's Disease.

2 Data, evaluation splits, metrics

2.1 Dataset

Ninety four participants were included from two observational cohorts (NCT01412125 and NCT03119246) in this ancillary study at the Hospital Henri-Mondor Créteil, France): 72 people tested with a number of CAG repeats on the Huntingtin gene above 35 (CAG > 35), and 22 Healthy Controls (C). Mutant Huntington gene carriers were considered premanifest if they both score less than five at the Total Motor score (TMS) and their Total functional capacity (TFC) equals 13 (Tabrizi et al., 2009) using the Unified Huntington Disease Rating Scale (UHDRS). All participants signed an informed consent and conducted an interview with an expert psychologist. Therefore in the diarization setting, there are two roles in each interview: a *Psychologist* and an *Interviewee*. The speech data were annotated with Seshat (Titeux* et al., 2020) and Praat (Boersma et al., 2002) softwares. The dataset is composed of $K = 94$ interviews $\mathcal{I}_{1...K}$. We designed a new way to split of speech dataset to compare different diarization approaches: an end-to-end Speaker Role Recognition model and a Speaker Enrollment pipeline (See Figure 2). The dataset is split in three sets which we refer to *meta-train set* M_{train}, *meta-dev set* M_{dev} and *meta-test set* M_{test} with the ratio of 60%, 20%, and 20%, respectively. Interview $I \in \mathcal{I}_{1...K}$ is composed of N_I segments $I = \{U_0, U_2, \ldots, U_{N_I}\}$. Each segment U_i is pronounced by a speaker s_i. We summarized the corpus statistics in Table 1.

Each interview I in the *meta-dev* and *meta-test* is split in two sets which we refer *dev set* X_{dev} and *test set* X_{test}. X_{test} is always kept fixed through all experiments, and we study the influence of the size of the X_{dev} based on T_{dev} that filters the segments (cf Figure 2).

All the data from the *meta-train* set M_{train} is used to train or fine-tune the neural network models for voice activity detection, speaker change detection, speaker role recognition, and speaker enrollment. The dev set X_{dev} of the *meta-dev* set M_{dev} and the dev set X_{dev} of the *meta-test* set M_{test} are only used for the speaker enrollment experiments, to build the template representation of each speakers. The results on the test set X_{test} of the *meta-dev* set M_{dev} are used to select all the hyper-parameters and select the best model for each experiment. The final comparison is done with the test set X_{test} of the *meta-test* set M_{test}.

Figure 2: Illustration of the data split with 4 interviews. Each line I_i represents an interview between the Interviewee and the Psychologist. The elevation of each row indicates 'who speaks when'. The segments can overlap.

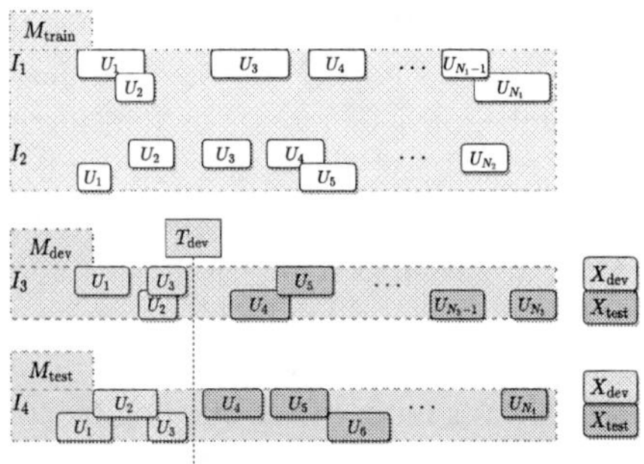

Table 1: Corpus statistics. P stands for Psychologist. IT stands for Interviewee. *Dur* stands for Duration and reported in hour. Durations are reported in hours.

	M_{train}	M_{dev}	M_{test}
#Interviews	57	18	19
#Segments IT	21400	7503	7788
#Segments P	4184	1381	1517
Dur Role IT	7.65	3.02	3.21
Dur Role P	3.54	1.14	1.15
Dur Overlap	1.10	0.50	0.45
C/preHD/HD	13/11/33	4/4/10	5/3/11

2.2 Metrics

To compare final performance of each approach, we use the Identification Error Rate (IER) taking into account both the segmentation and confusion errors. IER is obtained with `pyannote.metrics` (Bredin, 2017):

$$\text{IER} = \frac{T_{\text{false alarm}} + T_{\text{missed detection}} + T_{\text{confusion}}}{T_{\text{Total}}}$$

The $\frac{T_{\text{confusion}}}{T_{\text{Total}}}$ component in the IER is related to the Miss-classification Rate (MR%) used in Speaker Role Recognition study (Flemotomos et al., 2019), which is based on Frames and not duration of the turns. We compared the different approaches as a function of the size of the enrollment T_{dev} in Figure 3.

3 Methods

3.1 Speaker Role Recognition

We adapted the approach from (Lavechin et al., 2020) for the Speaker Role Recognition. We trained on M_{train} a unique model to detect each role (Psychologist,Interviewee), and selects the best epoch on M_{dev}. This is a multi-label multi-class segmentation problem. A threshold parameter for each role is optimized on the Meta-dev set M_{dev} for the two output units of the model. Therefore the two classes can be activated at the same time, i.e. we can also detect overlapped speech. To solve and model this task, we used SincNet filters (Ravanelli and Bengio, 2018) to obtain adapted speech features vectors from the audio signal. The SincNet output is fed to a stack of 2 bi-recurrent LSTM layers with hidden size of 128, then pass to a stack of 2 feed-forward layers of size 128 before a final decision layer. We used a binary cross-entropy loss and a cyclic scheduler as training procedure. The hyper-parameters to train our model can be found here [1].

3.2 Speaker enrollment protocol

The Speaker enrollment protocol can be decomposed into four tasks: (1) Voice Activity Detection (2) Speaker Change Detection, (3) Enrollment, (4) Identification. We extended the speech processing toolkit from (Bredin et al., 2020) `pyannote.audio` to run our experiments. Clinical laboratories can not all re-train in-domain speech processing models due to data scarcity or a lack of computational resources. Therefore, we evaluated pretrained models on open-source datasets and transfer models on our dataset to evaluate these out-of-domain performances with real clinical conversational conditions.

3.2.1 Voice Activity Detection

The first step is the Voice Activity Detection (VAD), i.e. obtain the speech segments in the audio signal. It can be modeled as an audio sequence labeling task. There are 2 classes (Speech or Non-Speech). The VAD labels for each interview I are the presence or not of a segment U_i at time t.

The model can be used already *Pretrained* or *Retrained* on the meta-train set M_{train} of our dataset. We choose the DIHARD dataset (Ryant et al., 2019) as a potential pretrained dataset as it contains multiple source domain data (clinical interviews among them). When trained from scratch, the training is done for 200 pyannote epochs and the model is selected on the Meta-dev M_{dev}. The model is also composed of SincNet filters with 2 bi-recurrent LSTM layers and 2 feed-forward layers. The full

[1] `https://tinyurl.com/etfrky3w`

specifications can be found here[2].

3.2.2 Speaker Change Detection

The second step is the Speaker Change Detection (SCD), i.e. obtain the moment when one of a speaker starts or stops talking. It can aslo be modeled as an audio sequence labeling task. There are 2 classes (Change or No-Change). The SCD labels for each interview I are the start or end of a segment U_i at time t. We also compared *Pretrained* on DIHARD and *Retrained* models. We used the same model as for the Voice Activity Detection. The full specifications can be found here.

Based on VAD and SCD outputs, for each Interview I we obtain a set of N_I' candidates speaker-homogeneous segments $\{\hat{U}_1, \dots \hat{U}_{N_I'}\}$.

3.2.3 Enrollment

In the enrollment stage, we need to get a Speaker Embedding function f_θ for our specific task. We combined SincNet filters and the X-vector architecture (Snyder et al., 2017) as in (Bredin et al., 2020). For finetuning, we froze all layers and finetuned the last layer. We used the VoxCeleb2 dataset (Nagrani et al., 2017) as a pretraining dataset as it contains a diverse distribution of speakers and recording conditions.

Then, we used the set of segments from the dev set X_{dev} of the *meta-dev* and *meta-test* to build a template vector m_j for each speaker j in the interview I. X_{dev} contain a set of segments $U_{\text{enrollment speaker } j}$ from each speaker j. The start of each segment $U_{\text{enrollment speaker } j}$ needs to be smaller than T_{dev}. We computed the average of the representations for each speaker j:

$$m_j = \frac{1}{|U_{\text{enrollment speaker } j}|} \sum_{U \in U_{\text{enrollment speaker } j}} f_\theta(U) \tag{1}$$

In principle, the more data you have to build template of each speaker, the easier it is to distinguish them. Thus, we studied the effect of the size of the enrollment based on the parameter $T_{dev} \in (90s, 100s, \dots, 180s)$ to build the template m_j (Larcher et al., 2014).

3.2.4 Identification

For the identification stage, we use the function f_θ and the different representation m_j of the speakers from the enrollment stage. We used the following

[2] https://tinyurl.com/44677f7c

Figure 3: Identification Error Rates for the different combination of approaches on the test set X_{test} of the meta-test set M_{test} as a function of the size of the enrollment parameter T_{dev}. *Spk Emb.*, *VAD,SCD* stand for Speaker Embedding, Voice Activity Detection and Speaker Change Detection. Best performance of each approach is displayed at the best T_{dev}.

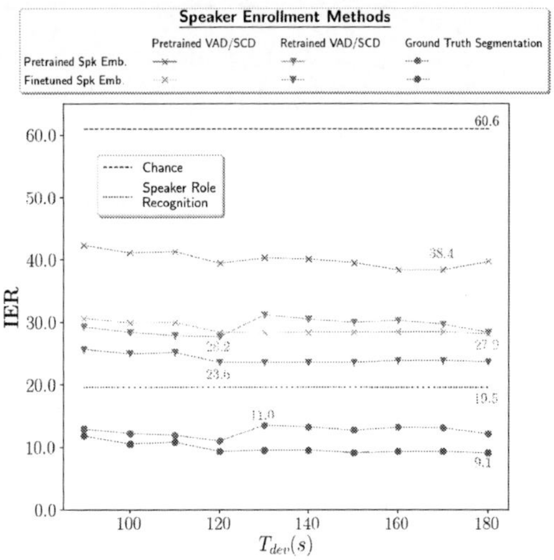

cosine distance D to build a scoring function and compare each segment $\hat{U} \in \{\hat{U}_1, \dots \hat{U}_{N_I'}\}$ to each template m_j:

$$D(\hat{U}, m_j) = \frac{1}{2}\left(1 - \frac{f_\theta(\hat{U})^\top m_j}{\left[\|f_\theta(\hat{U})\| \, \|m_j\|\right]}\right) \tag{2}$$

$$\text{argmin}_j \, D(\hat{U}, m_j) : \text{Selects Speaker } j \tag{3}$$

In addition, we analysed topline performance of the speaker embedding models when the Ground Truth Segmentation is provided. Finally, we computed a chance baseline based on speaker Enrollment by randomly permutating all the cosine distances. Spearman correlation is computed to compare clinical markers extracted from our best system to ground truth extractions (Figures 4 and 5).

4 Results and discussions

Figure 3 shows results in term of IER for the different approaches. Both approaches greatly improved over chance. If we consider pipelines solving both segmentation and identification, our best performance is obtained using the Speaker Role Recognition approach with IER=19.5% while the Speaker

Table 2: Speaker Role Recognition Ablation study: Identification Error Rates on the test set X_{test} of the meta-test set M_{test} as a function of the percentage of interview in the meta-train set M_{train}. MD stands for Missed detection, FA for False Alarm and Conf. for Confusion

% of M_{train}	MD	FA	Conf.	IER
10%	8.0	14.5	3.9	26.5
20%	7.8	12.4	3.8	24.0
50%	7.5	10.4	2.5	20.7
100%	7.1	10.2	2.3	19.5

Figure 4: Ratio of Silence from the Ground truth segmentation and from the best Speaker role recognition pipeline.

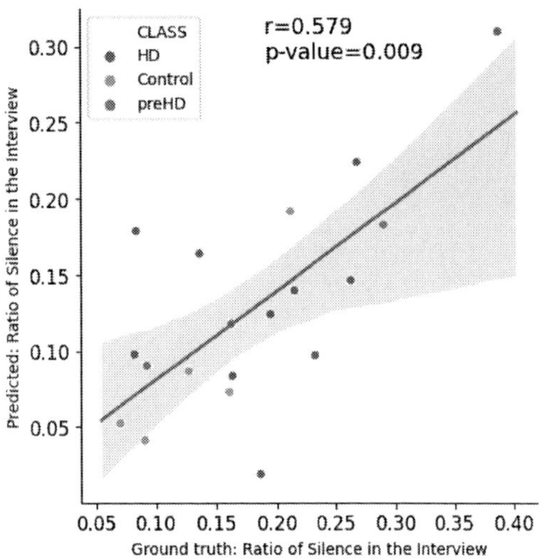

Enrollment Protocol obtained at best IER=23.6% at $T_{dev} = 120s$, with Retrained VAD/SCD models and Finetuned Speaker Embedding. Even though, the Speaker Enrollment protocol has per-speaker templates, it is not surpassing the Speaker Role Recognition approach. The topline with Ground Truth Segmentation (IER=9.1%) indicated that Speaker Enrollment could benefit greatly from a better detection of speaker-homogeneous turns. Errors of Speaker Enrollment are accumulated through the steps and can not be recovered, while Speaker Role Recognition takes advantage of solving all steps together in an end-to-end approach. Increasing the size of the Template Enrollment m_j for each speaker with T_{dev} lead to slight improvements to all Speaker Enrollment methods. The finetuning of the X-vector speaker embedding model with in-domain is especially crucial (ex: Based on retrained VAD/SCD the IER decreases from 28.2%

Figure 5: Standard Deviations (SD) of the Duration of Utterances of Interviewees from the Ground truth segmentation and the best Speaker role recognition system.

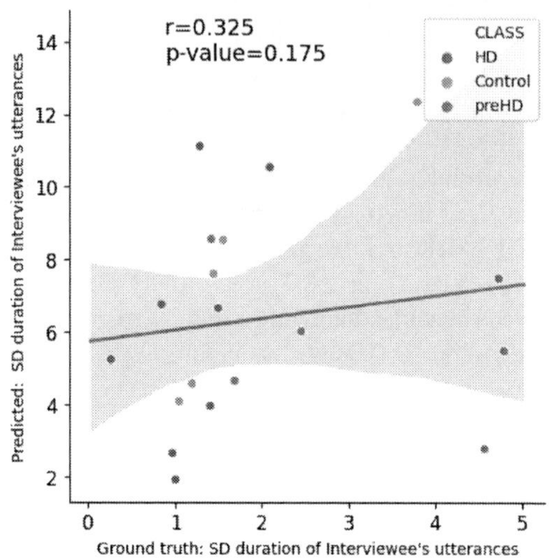

to 23.6%). We ran an additional ablation experiment (Table 2) for the Speaker Role Recognition to measure the amount of data necessary. This ablation study informed us on the necessary amount of data to reach certain level of performance. Even though models are better than Chance, we found out that at least 50% of our dataset (28 Interviews) is necessary to outperform the Speaker Enrollment Protocol pipeline (IER of 20.7% vs 23.6%). The analysis of the pattern of errors showed that the most important component is the False Alarm (FA), and a tenfold increase in dataset size allows to gain 4 points of FA. Therefore, most of the errors come from the voice activity detection part of the system. One of our hypothesis is that the system is confused by too much ambient noises from the hospital environment and thus potentially trigger too much positive presence of speech.

In previous studies in Huntington's Disease (Vogel et al., 2012; Perez et al., 2018), the Ratio of Silence and Statistics on utterances were informative to distinguish between classes of Individuals. These speech markers can be extracted directly from the predictions of the Speaker Role Recognition outputs. We computed the Ratio of Silence and the Standard Deviation of Duration of Utterances on the test set of the Meta-test set M_{test}. This computation was done both from the Ground Truth Segmentation and the segmentation provided by the Speaker role recognition system (Figures 4, 5. We observed that the automatic system outputs behaved differently as a function of clinical marker. The Ratio of Silence was better predicted (significant spearman correlation of $r = 0.579, p = 0.009$) than the SD of Duration of Utterances (non significant spearman correlation of $r = 0.325, p = 0.175$). One potential interpretation of our results is that the difference between the ratio and the standard deviation reveals that our pipeline is great overall to obtain summary statistics of the interview, but its precision at the turn-taking level is not sufficient to obtain turn statistics. Some bias of the predictive system might not hurt the IER metric but hurt the reliability of some clinical measures.

5 Conclusion and future work

Detection and Identification of speaker turns are fundamental problems in speech processing, especially in healthcare applications. While works studying these problems in isolation has provided valuable insights, in this work, we showed that Speaker Role Recognition was the most suitable approach for Interviewees at different stages of Huntington's Disease. For future work, we plan to investigate the use of these methods to derive robust biomarkers automatically and compare them to more classic approaches (Riad et al., 2020; Perez et al., 2018; Romana et al., 2020).

References

Sharon Ash and Murray Grossman. 2015. Why study connected speech production. *Cognitive neuroscience of natural language use*, pages 29–58.

Benjamin Bigot, Julien Pinquier, Isabelle Ferrané, and Régine André-Obrecht. 2010. Looking for relevant features for speaker role recognition. In *Eleventh Annual Conference of the International Speech Communication Association*.

Paul Boersma et al. 2002. Praat, a system for doing phonetics by computer. *Glot international*, 5.

Hervé Bredin. 2017. pyannote.metrics: a toolkit for reproducible evaluation, diagnostic, and error analysis of speaker diarization systems. In *Interspeech*, Stockholm, Sweden.

Hervé Bredin, Ruiqing Yin, Juan Manuel Coria, Gregory Gelly, Pavel Korshunov, Marvin Lavechin, Diego Fustes, Hadrien Titeux, Wassim Bouaziz, and Marie-Philippe Gill. 2020. Pyannote. audio: neural building blocks for speaker diarization. In *ICASSP*, pages 7124–7128. IEEE.

Shaojin Ding, Quan Wang, Shuo-Yiin Chang, Li Wan, and Ignacio-Lopez Moreno. 2020. Personal vad: Speaker-conditioned voice activity detection. In *Proc. Odyssey 2020 The Speaker and Language Recognition Workshop*, pages 433–439.

Nikolaos Flemotomos, Panayiotis Georgiou, David C Atkins, and Shrikanth Narayanan. 2019. Role specific lattice rescoring for speaker role recognition from speech recognition outputs. In *ICASSP*, pages 7330–7334. IEEE.

Nikolaos Flemotomos, Pavlos Papadopoulos, James Gibson, and Shrikanth Narayanan. 2018. Combined speaker clustering and role recognition in conversational speech. *Proc. Interspeech 2018*, pages 1378–1382.

Paola García, Jesus Villalba, Hervé Bredin, Jun Du, Diego Castan, Alejandrina Cristia, Latane Bullock, Ling Guo, Koji Okabe, Phani Sankar Nidadavolu, et al. 2019. Speaker detection in the wild: Lessons learned from jsalt 2019.

Simon Graf, Tobias Herbig, Markus Buck, and Gerhard Schmidt. 2015. Features for voice activity detection: a comparative analysis. *EURASIP Journal on Advances in Signal Processing*, 2015(1):91.

Georg Heigold, Ignacio Moreno, Samy Bengio, and Noam Shazeer. 2016. End-to-end text-dependent speaker verification. In *ICASSP*, pages 5115–5119. IEEE.

Wolfram Hinzen, Joana Rosselló, Cati Morey, Estela Camara, Clara Garcia-Gorro, Raymond Salvador, and Ruth de Diego-Balaguer. 2018. A systematic linguistic profile of spontaneous narrative speech in presymptomatic and early stage huntington's disease. *Cortex*, 100:71–83.

Nithin Rao Koluguri, Manoj Kumar, So Hyun Kim, Catherine Lord, and Shrikanth Narayanan. 2020. Meta-learning for robust child-adult classification from speech. In *ICASSP 2020-2020 IEEE International Conference on Acoustics, Speech and Signal Processing (ICASSP)*, pages 8094–8098. IEEE.

Rimita Lahiri, Manoj Kumar, Somer Bishop, and Shrikanth Narayanan. 2020. Learning domain invariant representations for child-adult classification from speech. In *ICASSP 2020-2020 IEEE International Conference on Acoustics, Speech and Signal Processing (ICASSP)*, pages 6749–6753. IEEE.

Anthony Larcher, Kong Aik Lee, Bin Ma, and Haizhou Li. 2014. Text-dependent speaker verification: Classifiers, databases and rsr2015. *Speech Communication*, 60:56–77.

Marvin Lavechin, Ruben Bousbib, Hervé Bredin, Emmanuel Dupoux, and Alejandrina Cristia. 2020. An open-source voice type classifier for child-centered daylong recordings. *arXiv preprint arXiv:2005.12656*.

Katie Matton, Melvin G McInnis, and Emily Mower Provost. 2019. Into the wild: Transitioning from recognizing mood in clinical interactions to personal conversations for individuals with bipolar disorder. *Proc. Interspeech*, pages 1438–1442.

Arsha Nagrani, Joon Son Chung, and Andrew Zisserman. 2017. Voxceleb: a large-scale speaker identification dataset. *Telephony*, 3:33–039.

Matthew Perez, Wenyu Jin, Duc Le, Noelle Carlozzi, Praveen Dayalu, Angela Roberts, and Emily Mower Provost. 2018. Classification of huntington disease using acoustic and lexical features. In *INTERSPEECH*, volume 2018, pages 1898–1902.

Mirco Ravanelli and Yoshua Bengio. 2018. Speaker recognition from raw waveform with sincnet. In *Spoken Language Technology Workshop (SLT)*, pages 1021–1028. IEEE.

Rachid Riad, Hadrien Titeux, Laurie Lemoine, Justine Montillot, Jennifer Hamet Bagnou, Xuan Nga Cao, Emmanuel Dupoux, and Anne-Catherine Bachoud-Lévi. 2020. Vocal markers from sustained phonation in huntington's disease. *arXiv preprint arXiv:2006.05365*.

A Romana, J Bandon, N Carlozzi, A Roberts, and EM Provost. 2020. Classification of manifest huntington disease using vowel distortion measures. In *Interspeech*, volume 2020, pages 4966–4970.

Neville Ryant, Kenneth Church, Christopher Cieri, Alejandrina Cristia, Jun Du, Sriram Ganapathy, and Mark Liberman. 2019. The second dihard diarization challenge: Dataset, task, and baselines. *Proc. Interspeech*, pages 978–982.

Ashtosh Sapru and Fabio Valente. 2012. Automatic speaker role labeling in ami meetings: recognition of formal and social roles. In *ICASSP*, pages 5057–5060. IEEE.

David Snyder, Daniel Garcia-Romero, Daniel Povey, and Sanjeev Khudanpur. 2017. Deep neural network embeddings for text-independent speaker verification. *Proc. Interspeech*, pages 999–1003.

Sarah J Tabrizi, Douglas R Langbehn, Blair R Leavitt, Raymund AC Roos, Alexandra Durr, David Craufurd, Christopher Kennard, Stephen L Hicks, Nick C Fox, Rachael I Scahill, et al. 2009. Biological and clinical manifestations of huntington's disease in the longitudinal track-hd study: cross-sectional analysis of baseline data. *The Lancet Neurology*, 8(9):791–801.

Hadrien Titeux*, Rachid Riad*, Xuan-Nga Cao, Nicolas Hamilakis, Kris Madden, Alejandrina Cristia, Anne-Catherine Bachoud-Lévi, and Emmanuel Dupoux. 2020. Seshat: A tool for managing and verifying annotation campaigns of audio data. In *LREC*, Marseille. * Equal contribution.

Adam P Vogel, Christopher Shirbin, Andrew J Churchyard, and Julie C Stout. 2012. Speech acoustic markers of early stage and prodromal huntington's disease: a marker of disease onset? *Neuropsychologia*, 50(14):3273–3278.

Producing Standard German Subtitles for Swiss German TV Content

Johanna Gerlach, Jonathan Mutal, Pierrette Bouillon
FTI, University of Geneva, Switzerland
johanna.gerlach, jonathan.mutal, pierrette.bouillon@unige.ch

Abstract

In this study we compare two approaches (neural machine translation and edit-based) and the use of synthetic data for the task of translating normalised Swiss German ASR output into correct written Standard German for subtitles, with a special focus on syntactic divergences. Results suggest that NMT is better suited to this task and that relatively simple rule-based generation of synthetic data could be a valuable approach for cases where little training data is available and transformations are simple.

1 Introduction

In Switzerland, two thirds of the population speak Swiss German, which is primarily a spoken language with many regional dialects. Swiss German has no standardised written form (Honnet et al., 2018), thus written communication relies on Standard German. Swiss German is widely used on Swiss TV, for example in news reports, interviews or talk shows. In order to make these contents accessible to people who cannot understand spoken Swiss German, either due to hearing impairments, or because they only understand Standard German, these TV programs need to be subtitled in Standard German. For daily TV content, where large amounts of subtitles need to be produced within a short time frame and in a cost-effective manner, being able to automate the subtitling process would be advantageous. The PASSAGE project, which is the context of the present study, focuses on this task.

Subtitling can be automated by combining automatic speech recognition (ASR) with intralingual machine translation to improve the output to achieve compliance with subtitling standards (Buet and Yvon, 2021). In the PASSAGE project a first ASR step is used to produce a normalised transcription of spoken Swiss German, keeping the original syntax and expressions but only using Standard German words. In a second step, a neural machine translation (NMT) and an edit-based approach are explored to transform this normalised transcription into correct written Standard German (see Figure 1 for an example). To achieve this, multiple issues must be dealt with: ASR errors, incorrect detection of sentence boundaries, features related to spontaneous spoken language, such as dysfluencies or informal language, and finally the syntactic divergences between Swiss German and Standard German (Scherrer, 2011; Arabskyy et al., 2021).

Spoken Swiss German:
und d'Regierig hät no wiiteri Idee zum d'Stüüre abetue.

Normalised transcription (ideal ASR result):
Und die Regierung hat noch weitere Ideen zum die Steuern senken

Standard German:
Und die Regierung hat noch weitere Ideen, um die Steuern zu senken.

Figure 1: Example of the subtitling steps

In the present study, we focus on the second step, and more specifically on the systems' ability to transform Swiss German syntactic phenomena into their Standard German counterparts. We compare different approaches and investigate whether additional synthetic training data targeting these phenomena can improve the models. To evaluate the systems' performance on this task, we perform human evaluations of several test suites.

The paper is structured as follows, Section 2 introduces the syntactic phenomena we have focused on, Section 3 presents the data and architectures used, followed by Section 4 which describes the evaluation approach. Results are given in Section 5. Section 6 presents our conclusions and directions for future work.

Ninth Workshop on Speech and Language Processing for Assistive Technologies (SLPAT-2022), pages 37 - 43

Corpus	Segments	Words
GSW_NORM	98,126	2,630,824
DE (original subtitles)	101,150	1,414,744
DE_PE	20,634	347,232
GSW_NORM-DE	70,374	1,265,846 - 871,435
sDE_PE	4,418	94,194 - 94,065
sDE	13,896	223,146 - 221,944

Table 1: Overview of the data sets. GSW_NORM-DE was automatically aligned

2 Syntactic divergences between Swiss German and Standard German

The syntactic differences between Swiss German and Standard German can be classified into two main types: features related to the mainly spoken usage of Swiss German on one hand and dialect-specific features on the other (Scherrer, 2011). The latter are language phenomena involving among others the positioning of verbal forms, the construction of clauses or the use of cases and pronouns. These phenomena also differ from region to region (Glaser and Bart, 2021), thus the TV content, which includes transcripts of speakers from all regions of German speaking Switzerland, covers a large number of variations. For this study, we have focused on a subset of phenomena that occur in our corpora and that require different transformations:

- Adjective phrases with intensity adverbs often present different determiner usage than in Standard German, with the determiner placed after the adverb, or doubled. (advArtAdj)
- The verb *tun* 'do' used as an auxiliary with a trailing infinitive, referred to as *tun-periphrase*, is very common in many dialects and in spoken German, but is considered informal, and therefore is not used in subtitles. (tun)
- The particles *für* or *zum* are used to introduce final clauses instead of the Standard German complementiser *um ... zu* 'in order to'. (umZu)
- Reversed verb order compared to Standard German, often referred to as *verb raising* (for an overview, see Wurmbrand, 2017) occurs in different cases, e.g. in subordinate clauses the modal verb is placed before the infinitive, or the auxiliary precedes the participle. (verbsAuxPP and verbsModalInf)
- The uninflected particle *wo* is often used instead of nominative and accusative relative pronouns. (wo)

See Table 5 in the Appendix for examples.

3 Data and systems

In this section we describe the initial data that were provided to build the systems, the aligned and synthetic corpora that were derived from these data, and the different architectures that we have used.

3.1 Data

Table 1 summarises the corpora with the number of segments and words. Initially SRF (Schweizer Radio und Fernsehen) provided the following data for several TV shows:

GSW_NORM: normalised human transcriptions of Swiss German speech, keeping the original syntax and expressions but using German words. These data were created to train the Swiss German speech recogniser and correspond to an ideal ASR result.

DE: the original Standard German subtitles of the TV shows, not aligned with the transcriptions.

Based on these data, we created three aligned corpora used for system training:

GSW_NORM-DE_PE: this corpus was produced by manual post-editing of GSW_NORM into Standard German.

GSW_NORM-DE: this corpus was aligned automatically using (Plüss et al., 2021) modified to take as input GSW_NORM instead of speech. The alignment finds similar word chunks between GSW_NORM and DE which are then post processed to reconstruct sentences based on punctuation. The result has not been validated manually and therefore could contain errors.

sDE_PE and sDE: Since the training data for this task is scarce, we have chosen to generate synthetic parallel data specifically for the syntactic phenomena described in Section 2 (Lee and Seneff, 2008; Hassan et al., 2017; Lample et al., 2018). To this end, we have used the SpaCy toolkit's Matcher[1] to create transformation rules that identify syntactic patterns in Standard German text based on sequences of tokens, POS or morphological features, and transform these into the corresponding Swiss German patterns, e.g. by changing word order or verbs forms. We have applied these rules to the two available Standard German corpora, DE_PE and DE. Table 2 provides an overview of the synthetic data.

Finally, our project partner recapp [2] provided ASR output for a subset of the TV shows. This was used for the evaluations described in section 4.

3.2 Systems

In this study we compare the performance of four systems based on two approaches: NMT and edit-based.

NMT: Transformer architecture with copy attention that is usually used in tasks where small changes are needed (Gehrmann et al., 2018). We trained the system with GSW_NORM-DE and specialised it with GSW_NORM-DE_PE (as suggested in Sennrich and Zhang, 2019). The purpose of this approach is to use a larger corpus with low quality segments for training to increase vocabulary coverage (Poncelas and Way, 2019) and then to specialise with high quality segments to eliminate noise.

Ed: Edit-based system that predicts types of edits instead of words (see more, Berard et al., 2017). We trained the system using GSW_NORM-DE and GSW_NORM-DE_PE, but since we did not achieve an optimal loss, the final version was trained using only GSW_NORM-DE_PE.

sNMT and sEd: Same architectures as NMT and Ed respectively, with addition of the synthetic data after the post-edited data (DE_PE) used for system specialisation. (see similar approach for grammar error correction, Wang et al., 2021).

[1]https://spacy.io/api/matcher

[2]https://recapp.ch/

	DE_PE	DE
orig. segments	20,634	101,196
advAdjArt	15	676
tun	26	2,167
umZu	21	1,088
verbsAuxPP	148	5,373
verbsModalInf	1,083	4,525
wo	187	5,204
transformed	4,418	13,896

Table 2: Synthetic training data: number of segments in the original corpora used for extraction, number of occurrences of each phenomenon in the synthetic data, final number of segments transformed by the rules and included in the synthetic training data

4 Evaluation methodology

The objective of our systems is to convert as many Swiss German syntactic phenomena as possible into Standard German, while not introducing any additional errors into the ASR output. To assess the systems' performance, we have therefore performed two human evaluations, as described in the following sections.

4.1 Syntactic divergences

To evaluate the systems' ability to transform the syntactic phenomena described in Section 2 into their Standard German counterparts, we have created a set of test suites. Starting with a corpus of 5,000 segments of unseen real ASR output, we have extracted sets of examples for each phenomenon. The extraction was performed semi-automatically in a two step process. In the first step, we extended the work by (Haberkorn, 2022) using the SpaCy toolkit's Matcher. Hand-crafted rules describing simple patterns are used to extract candidate sentences for each phenomenon. This extraction is not entirely accurate since the ASR output contains recognition errors as well as features of spontaneous speech (e.g. repetitions or incomplete phrases) that cannot be taken into account by simple rules. Therefore, in a second step, the extracted candidates were manually validated by a native German speaker to build test suites for each phenomenon, keeping up to 50 segments per phenomenon.

After processing with the four systems (NMT, Ed, sNMT and sEd), these test suites were annotated by two native German speakers, to determine whether the phenomena had been transformed cor-

test suite (N)	NMT	sNMT	Ed	sEd
advArtAdj (50)	38 (76%)	44 (90%)	1 (2%)	39 (78%)
tun (50)	14 (28%)	12 (24%)	2 (4%)	2 (4%)
umZu (31)	8 (26%)	10 (32%)	0 (0%)	3 (10%)
verbsAuxPP (31)	23 (74%)	31 (100%)	1 (3%)	19 (63%)
verbsModalInf (50)	45 (90%)	47 (94%)	9 (18%)	10 (20%)
wo (50)	43 (86%)	44 (88%)	35 (70%)	30 (60%)

Table 3: Results of the human evaluation of the test suites: number and fraction of segments where the selected phenomenon was transformed correctly

rectly or not. In this evaluation, only the phenomenon of interest was considered, disregarding the remainder of the segment. Disagreements between the two judges were reevaluated in order to reach a final common judgement.

4.2 Relevance of the systems' modifications

To evaluate the models' ability to make only relevant modifications, we have created a test corpus by randomly selecting a subset of 54 segments from the unseen ASR data. These were processed with the four systems, then word-level edits made by the systems (deletions and insertions) were highlighted automatically and annotated manually by two native German speakers. Edits that improved the output or performed a change that did not adversely affect the output, e.g. by replacing a word by a synonym, were marked as correct; edits that degraded the output were marked as incorrect. When improvement of the output requires replacement of one word by another, e.g. when the particle *wo* should be replaced by a pronoun, a deletion must be paired with a correct insertion to be of use. In these cases we have counted the deletion as correct only if the corresponding insertion was present and correct. Based on the edit counts, we calculated a precision score as the fraction of correct edits among all edits performed by each system.

5 Results

5.1 Syntactic divergences

Results of the evaluation of the test suites are reported in Table 3. We observe large differences between the test suites, which strongly suggests that some phenomena are easier to identify and correct than others. The percentage of correct transformations is substantially higher for the phenomena that only require reordering (such as advArtAdj and the two verb phenomena) than for those that require transformation of individual words (tun). For the more complex transformations, e.g. the replacement of the *tun-periphrase*, we observe partially correct transformations, with changed word order but unchanged verb forms.

Overall the NMT systems outperform the edit-based systems, without and with the synthetic training data.

5.2 Relevance of the systems' modifications

Results of the evaluation of precision are reported in Table 4. Overall we observe that the two NMT systems make more than twice as many edits as the Ed systems. In terms of precision, the NMT systems outperform the Ed systems. Agreement between the two annotators is moderate (Cohen's Kappa 0.566), suggesting that annotation is difficult and possibly ambiguous. Often segments include multiple overlapping issues such as ASR errors and dysfluencies which make sentences difficult to understand and edits difficult to assess.

For both approaches, NMT and edit-based, the addition of targeted synthetic data reduces the total number of edits. For NMT, the percentage of correct edits is slightly increased, while for the edit-based approach it is about the same, showing that the addition of synthetic data does not degrade overall precision. Further analysis is required to see if this reduced number of edits is related to the order in which the corpora are used for specialisation.

6 Conclusion

In this study we have compared two architectures and the use of synthetic data for the task of translating normalised Swiss German ASR output into correct written Standard German, with a special focus on syntactic differences. In terms of syntactic transformations, the NMT systems outperform the edit-based systems. We observe large differences between the studied phenomena, some being transformed more successfully than others. For NMT,

	NMT	sNMT	Ed	sEd
Total edits	201	145	69	45
Correct	173 / 153	127 / 122	52 / 52	34 / 25
Precision	0.861 / 0.761	0.876 / 0.841	0.754 / 0.754	0.756/ 0.556
#Edits/#Words	15.9%	10.6%	6.3%	4.0%

Table 4: Word-level edits performed by the systems on the corpus of 54 segments (1214 words) with correct edits and precision for the two annotators

the addition of targeted synthetic training data improves the results, producing a larger number of transformed phenomena while also having a slight positive impact on precision. These results suggest that the relatively simple rule-based generation of training data could be a valuable approach for cases where little training data is available and transformations are simple (e.g. inversion, insertion or replacement).

While results are promising, this study presents several limitations. We have only studied a subset of the syntactic phenomena that distinguish Swiss German from Standard German. Additionally, due to the constraints of human evaluation, only a limited set of data could be included. In terms of synthetic training data, we have only aimed to reproduce the syntactic phenomena, but not the orality markers which are very frequent in the ASR output the systems need to deal with. Finally, the evaluation in this study was focused on system performance in terms of performed edits. An ongoing evaluation with different target groups will show whether these syntactic changes have an impact on understandability, accessibility and general satisfaction.

Future work includes extending to other phenomena and specialising with different settings.

Acknowledgements

This project has received funding from the Initiative for Media Innovation based at Media Center, EPFL, Lausanne, Switzerland. We would also like to thank Melanie Arnold for their contribution to data annotation.

References

Yuriy Arabskyy, Aashish Agarwal, Subhadeep Dey, and Oscar Koller. 2021. Dialectal speech recognition and translation of swiss german speech to standard german text: Microsoft's submission to swisstext 2021 (short paper). In *Proceedings of the Swiss Text Analytics Conference 2021, Winterthur, Switzerland, June 14-16, 2021 (held online due to COVID19 pandemic)*, volume 2957 of *CEUR Workshop Proceedings*. CEUR-WS.org.

Alexandre Berard, Laurent Besacier, and Olivier Pietquin. 2017. Lig-cristal submission for the wmt 2017 automatic post-editing task. In *Proceedings of the Second Conference on Machine Translation*, page 623–629. Association for Computational Linguistics.

François Buet and François Yvon. 2021. Vers la production automatique de sous-titres adaptés à l'affichage. In *Traitement Automatique des Langues Naturelles*, pages 91–104, Lille, France. ATALA.

Sebastian Gehrmann, Yuntian Deng, and Alexander Rush. 2018. Bottom-up abstractive summarization. In *Proceedings of the 2018 Conference on Empirical Methods in Natural Language Processing*, page 4098–4109. Association for Computational Linguistics.

Elvira Glaser and Gabriela Bart. 2021. *Syntaktischer Atlas der deutschen Schweiz (SADS)*. A. Francke Verlag.

Veronika Christine Haberkorn. 2022. Automatic post-editing of subtitles - rule-based post-editing of subtitles from Swiss German to Standard German. Master's thesis, Faculty of translation and interpreting, University of Geneva.

Hany Hassan, Mostafa Elaraby, and Ahmed Tawfik. 2017. Synthetic data for neural machine translation of spoken-dialects. In *Proceedings of the 14th International Workshop on Spoken Language Translation*, pages 82–89, Tokyo, Japan.

Pierre-Edouard Honnet, Andrei Popescu-Belis, Claudiu Musat, and Michael Baeriswyl. 2018. Machine translation of low-resource spoken dialects: Strategies for normalizing swiss german. In *Proceedings of the Eleventh International Conference on Language Resources and Evaluation (LREC 2018)*. European Language Resources Association (ELRA).

Guillaume Lample, Alexis Conneau, Ludovic Denoyer, and Marc'Aurelio Ranzato. 2018. Unsupervised machine translation using monolingual corpora only. In *International Conference on Learning Representations*.

John Lee and Stephanie Seneff. 2008. Correcting misuse of verb forms. In *Proceedings of ACL-08: HLT*, pages 174–182, Columbus, Ohio. Association for Computational Linguistics.

Michel Plüss, Lukas Neukom, Christian Scheller, and Manfred Vogel. 2021. Swiss parliaments corpus, an automatically aligned swiss german speech to standard german text corpus. In *Proceedings of the Swiss Text Analytics Conference 2021, Winterthur, Switzerland, June 14-16, 2021 (held online due to COVID19 pandemic)*, volume 2957 of *CEUR Workshop Proceedings*. CEUR-WS.org.

Alberto Poncelas and Andy Way. 2019. Selecting artificially-generated sentences for fine-tuning neural machine translation. In *Proceedings of the 12th International Conference on Natural Language Generation*, page 219–228. Association for Computational Linguistics.

Yves Scherrer. 2011. Syntactic transformations for Swiss German dialects. In *Proceedings of the First Workshop on Algorithms and Resources for Modelling of Dialects and Language Varieties*, pages 30–38, Edinburgh, Scotland. Association for Computational Linguistics.

Rico Sennrich and Biao Zhang. 2019. Revisiting low-resource neural machine translation: A case study. In *Proceedings of the 57th Annual Meeting of the Association for Computational Linguistics*, page 211–221. Association for Computational Linguistics.

Yu Wang, Yuelin Wang, Kai Dang, Jie Liu, and Zhuo Liu. 2021. A comprehensive survey of grammatical error correction. *ACM Transactions on Intelligent Systems and Technology*, 12(5):1–51.

Susi Wurmbrand. 2017. Verb clusters, verb raising, and restructuring. In *The Wiley Blackwell Companion to Syntax, Second Edition*, pages 1–109. John Wiley & Sons, Ltd.

A Appendix

Phenomenon	Example	Conversion
advArtAdj	ein Land, wo **sehr einen** hohen Standard hat Punkto Sicherheit [. . .] → ein Land, wo **einen sehr** hohen Standard hat Punkto Sicherheit [. . .]	Reverse the order of adverb *sehr* and article *einen*
	Diese Mitarbeiter haben **einen sehr einen** hohen Ausbildungsstand → Diese Mitarbeiter haben **einen sehr** hohen Ausbildungsstand	Remove the doubled article *einen*
tun	Man **tut** sich solchen Fragen sicher nicht **verschliessen** → Man **verschliesst** sich solchen Fragen sicher nicht	Replace *tun* by the finite verb form *verschliesst* of the infinitive *verschliessen*
umZu	Man braucht eine Ausbildung **zum** sich können ablösen und von der Sozialhilfe wegkommen. → Man braucht eine Ausbildung, **um** sich ablösen **zu** können und von der Sozialhilfe wegkommen.	Replace the particle *zum* by the complementiser *um . . . zu*
verbsAuxPP	Freunde wo in der Intensivpflegestationen **sind gewesen** [. . .] → Freunde wo in der Intensivpflegestationen **gewesen sind** [. . .]	Reverse order of auxiliary *sind* and participle *gewesen*
verbsModalInf	Wir haben da das Gefühl gehabt, man muss den Leuten sagen, was man **kann machen** [. . .] → Wir haben da das Gefühl gehabt, man muss den Leuten sagen, was man **machen kann** [. . .]	Reverse order of modal *kann* and infinitive *machen*
wo	zum Beispiel diese Leute **wo** gelitten haben bei dem an Bergsturz → zum Beispiel diese Leute **die** gelitten haben bei dem an Bergstur	Replace uninflected particle *wo* by relative pronoun *die* that agrees in number and gender with the noun *Leute* to which it refers

Table 5: Examples of conversions from Swiss German patterns to Standard German patterns for the syntactic divergences included in the study. Examples are extracted from the test-suites. Only the sequences in bold have been edited, errors may subsist in the remainder of the segments.

Investigating the Medical Coverage of a Translation System into Pictographs for Patients with an Intellectual Disability

Magali Norré
CENTAL, UCLouvain, Belgium
FTI, UNIGE, Switzerland

Vincent Vandeghinste
Instituut voor de Nederlandse Taal
The Netherlands

Thomas François
CENTAL, UCLouvain, Belgium

Pierrette Bouillon
FTI, UNIGE, Switzerland

Abstract

Communication between physician and patients can lead to misunderstandings, especially for disabled people. An automatic system that translates natural language into a pictographic language is one of the solutions that could help to overcome this issue. In this preliminary study, we present the French version of a translation system using the Arasaac pictographs and we investigate the strategies used by speech therapists to translate into pictographs. We also evaluate the medical coverage of this tool for translating physician questions and patient instructions.

1 Introduction

Many people around the world face difficulties to communicate through speech. To overcome this challenge, disabled people, including persons with an Intellectual Disability (ID), resort to Augmentative and Alternative Communication (AAC) systems in different forms: objects, visual aids on paper or technologies (Beukelman and Mirenda, 1998). Both text and pictographs can be used in AAC for enhancing the communication and the social inclusion of individuals with ID.

Images are already used in various medical contexts to increase access to information and communication for all, e.g. in pharmacology on drug leaflets for improving the health literacy or in hospitals for facilitating the medical tourism (Nandy, 2019). In emergency settings, there are tools such as interpreters and communication technologies for allophones patients (Janakiram et al., 2021). However, they have drawbacks and are not designed for people with disabilities. Recent research focuses on medical applications with images for disabled patients, but does not use NLP techniques (Norré et al., 2021b), such as My Symptoms Translator (Alvarez, 2014) or the system of Wołk et al. (2017).

This paper focuses on the French version of a translation system using the Arasaac pictographs[1] (Norré et al., 2021b) and makes two contributions: investigates the strategies used by speech therapists for translating medical sentences into pictographs and evaluates the lexical coverage of the system. Section 2 summarizes related work on the translation systems with images and their evaluation. We describe our system in Section 3. Section 4 investigates translation strategies. Finally, we evaluate the medical coverage of our system in Section 5.

2 Related Work

Pictographs represent one or several concepts: object, verb, feeling, grammatical word, etc. There are several pictograph sets available, such as Sclera, Beta or Arasaac, which are specifically created for people with various disabilities. They can be seen as simplified languages (Sevens et al., 2017). Therefore, they have been used within AAC systems, but many relate to daily communication.

As regards the medical language, Glyph (Bui et al., 2012) – which is not an AAC application – automatically translates patient instructions from text into pictures with NLP and computer graphics techniques. The BabelDr system (Bouillon et al., 2021) proposes pictographs and allows to translate spoken medical utterances in various languages to communicate with migrants and deaf patients in hospitals. For people with ID, de Knegt et al. (2016a,b) designed a tool with pictographs, called STOP-ID, to aid the self-reporting of pain (affect, location, intensity and quality). The authors also tested the ability to recognize representations for vocabulary and pain of their tool in adults with ID.

The comprehension of single pictographs in context is increasingly evaluated with users: e.g. for the patient responses to medical questions (Norré et al., 2021a). However, most studies still rely on automated metrics used in MT such as BLEU

[1] `https://arasaac.org`

Ninth Workshop on Speech and Language Processing for Assistive Technologies (SLPAT-2022), pages 44 - 49
May 27, 2022 ©2022 Association for Computational Linguistics

(Papineni et al., 2002), NIST (Doddington, 2002), etc. to assess sentences automatically translated into pictographs (Sevens, 2018; Vaschalde et al., 2018; Norré et al., 2021b). Mihalcea and Leong (2008) tested sentences whose nouns and verbs had been automatically translated into pictures. Finally, some evaluations are also carried out by researchers, such as in Bui et al. (2012), which rated the correctness of 49 patient instructions converted with Glyph. More recently, Bulté et al. (2021) manually evaluated the comprehension and the lexical coverage of sentences generated into three pictographic languages by their translation system.

3 Translation System

Our system was originally designed for the online communication of people with ID and was hence optimised for social media context (Sevens, 2018). It translates texts written in four natural languages into any combination of four pictograph sets. This paper focuses on French and the medical domain with Arasaac pictographs (see Section 4), as there are fewer medical pictographs in the other sets.

The text to translate first undergoes shallow linguistic analysis: sentence detection, tokenization, POS-tagging and lemmatization with TreeTagger (Schmid, 1994), simple detection of multi-word expressions (MWE), processing of specific French phenomena based on rules and dictionaries (Norré et al., 2021b). Then, each word of the text can be translated through two routes: the semantic route and the direct route. In the semantic route, each word is looked up in the WOLF database (Sagot and Fišer, 2008), a French version of WordNet (Miller, 1995). If it is not found, hyperonym and antonym relations of WOLF are used to get substitute translation. For example, as there is no pictograph for *saumon* (salmon), the word is translated by its hyperonym *poisson* (fish). The word *infecter* (infect) does not have a pictograph and is translated by its antonym followed by the negative pictograph, *désinfecter non* (desinfect no). For the direct route, we build a dictionary for the pictographic language that contains the words not covered by WOLF (e.g., prepositions, pronouns, etc.). Pictograph filenames (i.e. French lemmas) are linked to their identifiers available on the Arasaac website. To choose the optimal path while converting a sequence of lemmas to a sequence of pictographs, we use a search algorithm A* (Vandeghinste et al., 2015).

Compared to our previous work (Norré et al., 2021b), various improvements were brought to our system. We updated our pictograph database with new pictographs from Arasaac API,[2] as more medical pictographs have been added due to the Covid pandemic. Several AAC systems with pictographs use a color coding system that informs about the syntactic category of the words represented. This makes it possible to improve the learning of vocabulary and therefore its use. We implemented the coding system of Fitzgerald (1949), which highlights the borders of pictographs with colors, depending on their POS: green for verbs, blue for adjectives, etc. At the beginning of sentences, we also generate a temporal pictograph for past and future tenses (see Figure 1), as Sevens et al. (2017). We added a WOLF relation: eng_derivative, to get similar concepts with a different POS tag, e.g. for the adjective *respiratoire* (breathing), our system translates it by the verb *respirer* (breathe). It is the equivalent of xpos_near_synonym relation in other WordNets. We will therefore call it the xpos relation in Section 5. Finally, we added simple rules of compression for different French phenomena found in our previous evaluation (deletion of some function words, auxiliaries, verb-subject inversion in questions, simplification of some imperative structures for patient instructions). These rules are based on an analysis of our system's output, the advice from a speech therapist and a syntactic analysis carried out on medical sentences from the BabelDr system with the Berkeley Neural Parser (Kitaev and Klein, 2018).[3]

4 Translation Strategies for Pictographs

As we aim to automatically translate physician questions and patient instructions into Arasaac pictographs, we ran into the issue of the lack of a large authentic medical corpora in pictographs built by AAC users and the lack of translation guidelines to create such as a corpus. Therefore, we have investigated the actual strategies used by speech therapists to carry out such translation. This section first describes the data to translate, then lists the different translation strategies observed.

4.1 Data Set

For our translation experiment, we used the Arasaac pictograph set, an open source set that is in-

[2]https://arasaac.org/developers/api

[3]https://github.com/nikitakit/self-attentive-parser

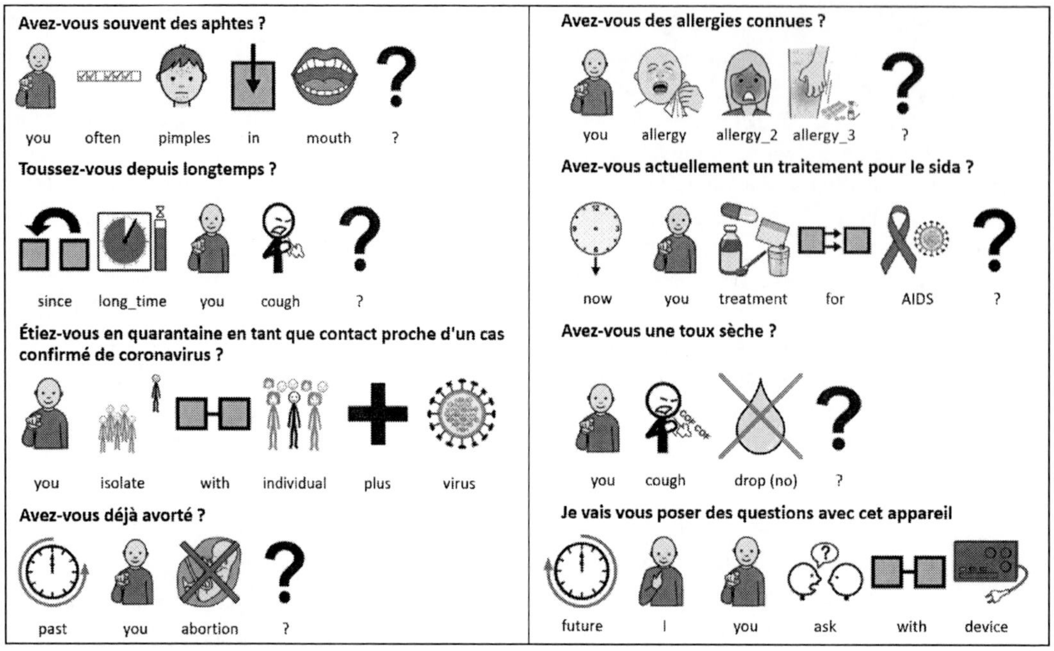

Figure 1: Examples of possible medical translations into Arasaac pictographs.

creasingly used by disabled people. This database includes over 12,000 pictographs in colours (also available in black and white and customizable online). Many domains (Paolieri and Marful, 2018), including communication in health sciences, are represented in this set. In November 2021, there were 1,126 medical pictographs grouped into 45 (sub)categories, such as medical procedures, covid-19, symptoms, etc. For the medical data to translate, we used French sentences of the BabelDr translation system (Bouillon et al., 2021), designed to facilitate communication between physicians and allophone patients. These data include physician questions, patient instructions, and greetings.

4.2 Translation Strategies

As Vandeghinste and Schuurman (2014) noted, a pictograph translation is not a literal translation. Various translation strategies can be used, the simpler one consisting in looking up each word lemma to translate in the pictograph set (Vaschalde, 2018). To uncover more sophisticated strategies, we asked a retired speech therapist – trainer and director of a Belgian AAC association – to manually translate 100 sentences from our medical data into Arasaac pictographs.

By comparing the original text and these sentences translated into pictographs, we noted at least 10 operations to improve the translation and the lexical coverage if a pictograph (filename) is missing: 1) deletion: delete some words of source sentence (e.g., articles, auxiliaries, etc.);[4] 2) insertion: if there is no pictograph for a (technical) term, insert a paraphrase with general concepts more easily comprehensible for patient (*aphtes: boutons dans bouche* | canker sores: pimples in mouth, as in Strasly et al. (2018) for translating sign language) or insert a clarification (*allergies connues: allergie allergie_2 allergie_3* | known allergies: allergy allergy_2 allergy_3); 3) moving: move one or several words (*toussez-vous depuis longtemps ?: depuis longtemps vous toussez ?* | cough you since long time ?: since long_time you cough ?); 4) synonym: replace by a synonym with an identical POS (*actuellement: maintenant* | currently: now); 5) hyperonym (*coronavirus: virus*); 6) hyponym (*personne: individu* | person: individual); 7) antonym (*sèche: goutte [non]* | dry: drop [no]); 8) POS change (*avorter: avortement* | abort: abortion); 9) compound2single: replace a MWE by a single word (*poser des questions: demander* | ask questions: ask); 10) replacement: replace one word with another with different root and/or POS, not by a synonym/hyperonym/etc. (*quarantaine: isoler* |

[4]The deletion depends on skill of user with ID. Note that removing all words by POS (e.g., adverbs) can change the meaning of sentences a lot (Vaschalde et al., 2018).

quarantine: isolate).

Figure 1 shows examples of expected medical translations into Arasaac pictographs.[5] Several translation operations can be combined in a sentence. These operations are already partially taken into account in the French version of the system we described in the previous section.

5 Preliminary Evaluation

We present the system tuning and an automated evaluation (Section 5.1), before the manual evaluation to assess the medical coverage (Section 5.2).

5.1 System Tuning and Automated Evaluation

For tuning and evaluation purposes, 150 additional medical sentences were manually translated into Arasaac by the authors. 60 sentences were used to tune the hyperparameters of the system (Vandeghinste et al., 2015) – related to WOLF relations, pictograph features and route preference – with a local hill climbing algorithm (5 trials of 50 iterations) using the BLEU metric (Papineni et al., 2002) as Norré et al. (2021b) on an email corpus.

	BLEU	WER	PER
- xpos relation	30.3 (2.3)	55.5 (2.1)	50.5 (1.9)
+ xpos relation	27.3 (2.2)	61.4 (2.6)	56.3 (2.5)

Table 1: System results on medical data for Arasaac: BLEU, WER and PER metrics (mean and std. dev.).

Then, we automatically evaluated the translation system on the remaining 90 sentences (Table 1). The BLEU scores are in line with our study (Norré et al., 2021b). For the French Text-to-Picto system, we got a BLEU score of 31.3 on a medical corpus for Arasaac, but with a largest reference corpus in which all the words had to be translated, including function words. Adding the xpos relation in our system (see Section 3) does not improve the results.

5.2 Manual Evaluation

Two experiments were carried out. We first calculated the number of untranslated words on 700 sentence transcripts of real physician questions, recorded with speech recognition of BabelDr system (Bouillon et al., 2021). We also evaluated 700 sentences, called canonicals, linked to each of these transcripts in the BabelDr system. Table 2 shows the number of untranslated types (and untranslated tokens in brackets). The use of xpos relation allows to translate more words even if we did not evaluate if all these translated words were correct.

	Transcripts	Canonicals
- xpos relation	126 (191)	102 (229)
+ xpos relation	110 (159)	81 (203)

Table 2: System results on medical data for Arasaac: number of untranslated types (and untranslated tokens).

As regards the lexical coverage, two authors of this paper manually evaluated 50 canonicals automatically generated with the system (without the xpos relation). They used UMLS concepts (Bodenreider, 2004) linked to these sentences to judge if the meaning was preserved. For each of the 103 concepts,[6] they annotated if the concepts were correctly translated into pictographs and by what type of representation (synonym, hyperonym or generic, hyponym or specific and polyseme). The Cohen's κ (Cohen, 1960) is 0.65, indicating that the agreement between both raters is substantial.

	Annotator 1	Annotator 2
Correct translation	62.1 (75.4)	71.8 (82.8)
No translation	37.8 (24.5)	28.1 (17.1)

Table 3: System results on medical data for Arasaac: lexical coverage (in %).

Table 3 shows the results of medical coverage by UMLS concept. The most used relation is synonymy. The annotators reported 5-6 hyperonyms (*nausée|diarrhée: symptomes* | nausea|diarrhea: symptoms), 2-5 hyponyms (*examen: examen des yeux* | examination: eye examination) and 3-4 polysemous words (*enceinte* means pregnant or speaker in French). There were also some MWE (*prise de sang* | blood test) incorrectly translated by two pictographs (*tenir sang* | grasp blood), but the MWE we had annotated with two synsets were correctly translated by a single pictograph (*mal à la tête* | headache). The untranslated words were mainly adjectives (*régulier* | regular) – more difficult to represent – and nouns (*type* | type). Figure 2 shows examples of system's outputs in Arasaac pictographs. The medical coverage can be still improved, especially the precision of the system, e.g. testing other lexical resources or NLP techniques that exploit the translation strategies into pictographs.

[5]The glosses are given using the English filenames of Arasaac pictographs. We added underscores and numbers.

[6]Or 187 concepts if we include the no UMLS concepts (e.g., pronouns and question marks). We also give results on this total in brackets in the table.

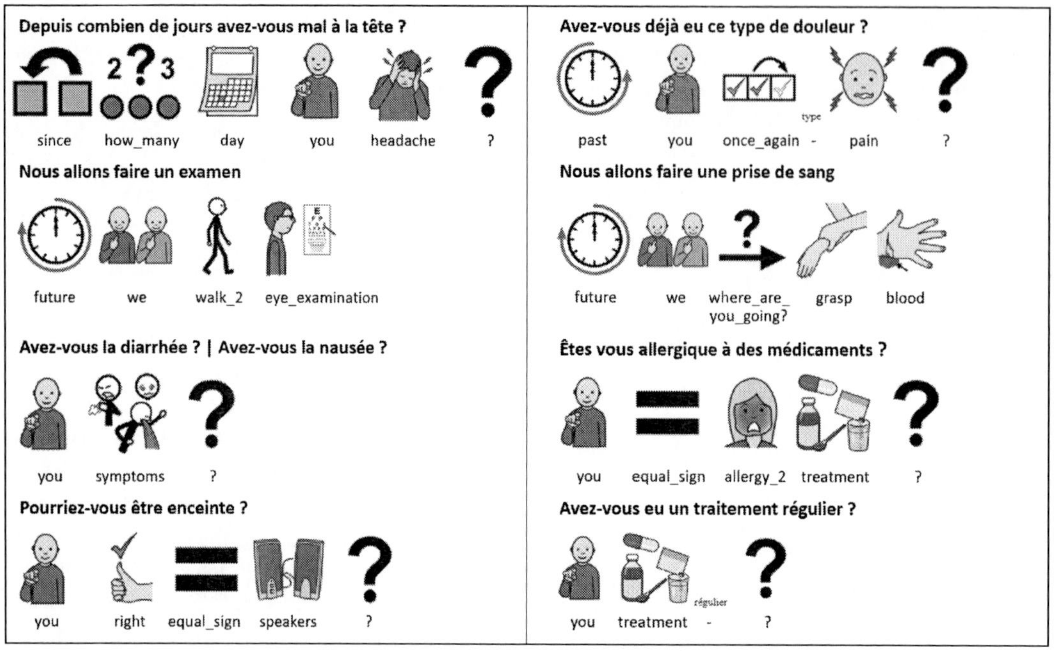

Figure 2: Examples of system's outputs in Arasaac.

6 Conclusion

We proposed an original way to investigate the medical coverage of our translation system from French into Arasaac pictographs using UMLS concepts. We also discussed the translation strategies into pictographs for medical sentences.[7] There is room for further improvement to specialize this system to the medical dialogue between physician and patients with ID. Some linguistic phenomena are not yet taken into account in the French system, such as the word sense disambiguation. Both the pictographic representations and the sentence comprehensibility into pictographs by the target users would need to be further investigated in context.

Acknowledgements

This work is also part of the PROPICTO project, funded by the Fonds National Suisse (N°197864) and the Agence Nationale de la Recherche (ANR-20-CE93-0005). The pictographs used are property of the Aragon Government and have been created by Sergio Palao to Arasaac. Aragon Government distributes them under Creative Commons License.

[7] The source code of the Text-to-Picto system, the manual and automated translations in Arasaac pictographs are available for the research community at the following address: https://github.com/VincentCCL/Picto.

References

Juliana Alvarez. 2014. Visual design. A step towards multicultural health care. *Arch Argent Pediatr*, 112(1):33–40.

David R. Beukelman and Pat Mirenda. 1998. *Augmentative and alternative communication*. Paul H. Brookes Baltimore.

Olivier Bodenreider. 2004. The Unified Medical Language System (UMLS): integrating biomedical terminology. *Nucleic acids research*, 32(suppl_1):D267–D270.

Pierrette Bouillon, Johanna Gerlach, Jonathan David Mutal, Nikolaos Tsourakis, and Hervé Spechbach. 2021. A speech-enabled fixed-phrase translator for healthcare accessibility. In *Proceedings of the 1st Workshop on NLP for Positive Impact*. Association for Computational Linguistics.

Duy Duc An Bui, Carlos Nakamura, Bruce E. Bray, and Qing Zeng-Treitler. 2012. Automated illustration of patients instructions. In *AMIA Annual Symposium Proceedings*, volume 2012, page 1158. American Medical Informatics Association.

Bram Bulté, Vincent Vandeghinste, Leen Sevens, Ineke Schuurman, and Frank Van Eynde. 2021. Can pictograph translation technologies facilitate communication and integration in migration settings? *Computational Linguistics in the Netherlands Journal*, 11:189–212.

Jacob Cohen. 1960. A coefficient of agreement for

nominal scales. *Educational and psychological measurement*, 20(1):37–46.

Nanda de Knegt, Frank Lobbezoo, Carlo Schuengel, Heleen M. Evenhuis, and Erik J. A. Scherder. 2016a. Self-Reporting Tool On Pain in People with Intellectual Disabilities (STOP-ID!): a Usability Study. *Augmentative and Alternative Communication*, 32(1).

Nanda de Knegt, Carlo Schuengel, Frank Lobbezoo, Corine M. Visscher, Heleen M. Evenhuis, Judith A. Boel, and Erik J. A. Scherder. 2016b. Comprehension of pictograms for pain quality and pain affect in adults with Down syndrome. *Journal of Intellectual & Developmental Disability*, 41(3):222–232.

George Doddington. 2002. Automatic evaluation of machine translation quality using n-gram co-occurrence statistics. In *Proceedings of the second international conference on Human Language Technology Research*, pages 138–145.

Edith Fitzgerald. 1949. *Straight language for the deaf: a system of instruction for deaf children*. Volta Bureau.

Antony Akash Janakiram, Pierrette Bouillon, Johanna Gerlach, Patricia Martha Hudelson Perneger, and Hervé Spechbach. 2021. J'ai de la peine à communiquer avec mon patient aux urgences. Quels sont les outils disponibles ? *Revue médicale suisse*, 7(739):995–998.

Nikita Kitaev and Dan Klein. 2018. Constituency parsing with a self-attentive encoder. *arXiv preprint arXiv:1805.01052*.

Rada Mihalcea and Chee Wee Leong. 2008. Toward communicating simple sentences using pictorial representations. *Machine translation*, 22(3):153–173.

George A. Miller. 1995. WordNet: A lexical database for English. *Communications of the ACM*, 38(11).

Ankita Nandy. 2019. Beyond words: Pictograms for Indian languages. *International Journal of Research in Science and Technology*, 9(1):19–25.

Magali Norré, Pierrette Bouillon, Johanna Gerlach, and Hervé Spechbach. 2021a. Evaluating the comprehension of Arasaac and Sclera pictographs for the BabelDr patient response interface. In *Proceedings of the 3rd Swiss Conference on Barrier-free Communication*, pages 55–63. ZHAW Zurich University of Applied Sciences.

Magali Norré, Vincent Vandeghinste, Pierrette Bouillon, and Thomas François. 2021b. Extending a Text-to-Pictograph System to French and to Arasaac. In *Proceedings of the International Conference on Recent Advances in Natural Language Processing (RANLP 2021)*, pages 1050–1059.

Daniela Paolieri and Alejandra Marful. 2018. Norms for a Pictographic System: the Aragonese Portal of Augmentative/Alternative Communication (ARASAAC) System. *Frontiers in psychology*, 9:2538.

Kishore Papineni, Salim Roukos, Todd Ward, and Wei-Jing Zhu. 2002. BLEU: A method for automatic evaluation of machine translation. In *Proceedings of the 40th annual meeting of the Association for Computational Linguistics*, pages 311–318.

Benoît Sagot and Darja Fišer. 2008. Building a free French WordNet from multilingual resources. In *OntoLex*, Marrakech, Morocco.

Helmut Schmid. 1994. Probabilistic part-of-speech tagging using decision trees. In *New methods in language processing*, page 154.

Leen Sevens. 2018. *Words Divide, Pictographs Unite: Pictograph Communication Technologies for People with an Intellectual Disability*. LOT, JK Utrecht, The Netherlands.

Leen Sevens, Vincent Vandeghinste, Ineke Schuurman, and Frank Van Eynde. 2017. Simplified text-to-pictograph translation for people with intellectual disabilities. In *International Conference on Applications of Natural Language to Information Systems*, pages 185–196. Springer.

Irene Strasly, Tanya Sebaï, Evelyne Rigot, Valentin Marti, Jesus Manuel Gonzalez, Johanna Gerlach, Hervé Spechbach, and Pierrette Bouillon. 2018. Le projet babelDr : rendre les informations médicales accessibles en Langue des Signes de Suisse Romande (LSF-SR). In *Proceedings of the 2nd Swiss Conference on Barrier-free Communication*, pages 92–96.

Vincent Vandeghinste and Ineke Schuurman. 2014. Linking pictographs to synsets: Sclera2Cornetto. In *Proceedings of the Ninth International Conference on Language Resources and Evaluation (LREC'14)*, volume 9, pages 3404–3410. ELRA, Paris.

Vincent Vandeghinste, Ineke Schuurman, Leen Sevens, and Frank Van Eynde. 2015. Translating text into pictographs. *Natural Language Engineering*, 23(2):217–244.

Céline Vaschalde. 2018. Génération automatique de pictogrammes à partir de la parole pour faciliter la mise en place d'une communication médiée. Master's thesis, Université d'Orléans.

Céline Vaschalde, Pauline Trial, Emmanuelle Esperança-Rodier, Didier Schwab, and Benjamin Lecouteux. 2018. Automatic pictogram generation from speech to help the implementation of a mediated communication. In *Proceedings of the 2nd Swiss Conference on Barrier-free Communication*.

Krzysztof Wołk, Agnieszka Wołk, and Wojciech Glinkowski. 2017. A cross-lingual mobile medical communication system prototype for foreigners and subjects with speech, hearing, and mental disabilities based on pictograms. *Computational and mathematical methods in medicine*, 2017.

On the Ethical Considerations of Text Simplification

Sian Gooding
Department of Computer Science and Technology
University of Cambridge
shg36@cam.ac.uk

Abstract

This paper outlines the ethical implications of text simplification within the framework of assistive systems. We argue that a distinction should be made between the technologies that perform text simplification and the realisation of these in assistive technologies. When using the latter as a motivation for research, it is important that the subsequent ethical implications be carefully considered. We provide guidelines for the framing of text simplification independently of assistive systems, as well as suggesting directions for future research and discussion based on the concerns raised.

Some philatelists say the committee that helps the postmaster general pick new stamps is favoring pop celebrities and fictional characters over cultural sites and historical figures, undermining a long tradition.
↓
Some philatelists (as stamp collectors are known) say the committee that helps pick new stamps is favoring pop stars and fictional characters. Such choices mean that cultural sites and historical figures are appearing less often. They say this results in the undermining of a long tradition.

Table 1: Example of manually simplified sentence from the Newsela Dataset (Xu et al., 2015)

1 Introduction

Assistive technology refers to the devices used to support or aid those living with disabilities (Preston, 2003). The intent behind such technologies is to increase independence and maximise societal participation for individuals (Borg et al., 2011).

There are many examples of assistive technology that rely on speech and natural language processing. For instance, sign language translation (Camgoz et al., 2018), pronunciation adaptation for disordered speech (Sriranjani et al., 2015) and synthesised voices for individuals with vocal disabilities (Veaux et al., 2013). *Text simplification* is an area of natural language processing concerned with the simplification of textual information and is often recognised as having assistive applications. Prior research in text simplification posits that such technology may be beneficial for audiences with reading difficulties or a range of disabilities such as dyslexia, aphasia or deafness.

However, currently the algorithms designed for text simplification are considered in isolation from their assistive applications, and there is subsequently little discussion on the ethical implications for the intended users. Text simplification research is often motivated by highlighting the audiences that could benefit from such tools, thereby coupling the technology with the assistive applications. Framing text simplification via the implications for assistive technology means that the ethical considerations cannot be easily separated from the technology used to generate the result. An issue which is commonly acknowledged in the assistive technology literature (Niemeijer et al., 2010).

There are many potential benefits of text simplification embedded in assistive technology, and both for service providers and service users, there are also a number of ethical issues that must be considered. In this paper, we will discuss the ethical considerations that arise from the embedding of text simplification within assistive technologies. Our aim is to encourage the discussion and consideration of these issues, as well as inform the design decisions of future assistive technologies that incorporate text simplification.

2 Background

Complete textual simplification requires many types of transformations which can be grouped into three categories: syntactic, lexical and conceptual (Siddharthan, 2014). Table 1 illustrates a range of simplification operations from these different

Ninth Workshop on Speech and Language Processing for Assistive Technologies (SLPAT-2022), pages 50 - 57

categories, a description of these is as follows:

Lexical simplification is concerned with reducing the complexity of words within a text (Paetzold and Specia, 2017; Gooding and Kochmar, 2019). In lexical simplification, complex words are identified and replaced with simpler alternatives. We observe an example of lexical simplification with the case of *celebrities* being simplified to *stars*.

Syntactic simplification aims to reduce the grammatical complexity of text by simplifying the syntactical structures. Examples of such transformations include the conversion of text from passive to active voice and dis-embedding relative clauses (Siddharthan, 2006a). In our example, multiple syntactic simplifications have taken place. One such simplification occurs where the subordinated clause '*...undermining a long tradition*' has been split into a separate sentence. Syntactic simplification often requires discourse preserving edits to maintain the coherence and cohesion of simplified text. For instance, the addition of '*They say...*' is necessary to convert the original relative clause into a grammatically correct and coherent sentence.

Finally, conceptual simplification focuses on the simplification of ideas or concepts within text. The example shows how the concept of *philatelist* has been simplified by providing an explanation of the term. This simplification technique is commonly referred to as elaboration, as the meaning of the concept has been elaborated on (Siddharthan, 2006a). Often, this strategy is used in cases where no alternative synonym would suffice, for instance with named entities.

Both syntactic and conceptual simplification contain parallels with the research area of *text summarization* as omitting peripheral or inappropriate information, as well as distilling complex concepts, is relevant for both. However, in simplification these processes can increase the length of the original text, whereas in summarization the goal is to constrain the length of the resulting summary.

In automatic text simplification, the aim is to transform text using the aforementioned operations, to allow individuals with differing comprehension levels access. This requires a fundamental understanding of what factors contribute to text complexity for differing audiences (Gooding et al., 2021b).

Early approaches to automated simplification were largely rule-based systems (Canning et al., 2000; Carroll et al., 1998a; Siddharthan, 2006b), with many prioritising syntactic operations, such as sentence splitting, deletion or reordering. However, some work combined lexical simplification with syntactic operations (Coster and Kauchak, 2011; Kauchak, 2013; Zhu et al., 2010). In recent years simplification has been viewed as a monolingual translation task (Kauchak, 2013; Zhang and Lapata, 2017; Zhu et al., 2010). These systems perform a number of simplification operations at once by aiming to translate *complex English* to *simple English*. Initial approaches attempt this with phrase-based machine translation (Coster and Kauchak, 2011; Wubben et al., 2012) while subsequent work has focused on neural machine translation techniques (Nisioi et al., 2017; Zhang and Lapata, 2017; Shardlow and Nawaz, 2019; Dong et al., 2019).

3 Risks and Harms

In this section we outline and discuss the potential risks and harms that arise from the integration of text simplification within assistive technology.

3.1 Intended Audience

As with many areas of research, the field of text simplification has converged on a partially boilerplate preamble outlining a set of motivations. Table 2 features extracts taken from a sample of recent text simplification papers. These papers were sampled by searching the ACL anthology for the term *text simplification* and ordering by most recent. We look specifically at sections outlining the audiences said to benefit from text simplification as a whole. Below, we consider the ethical implications of citing such audiences as a motivation for text simplification.

3.1.1 The Homogeneity Effect

As shown in Table 2, the audiences stated to benefit from text simplification are often listed together, namely non-native speakers, children, people with low literacy skills, people with reading disabilities or disabilities generally. Based on this, a reader may be given the impression that general purpose text simplification works adequately for all of the stated groups. Whereas in fact, there is evidence to show that text simplification may not be effective for second language learners (Young, 1999), that alternative strategies to simplification can be most effective for dyslexia (Rello et al., 2013a) and that automated text simplification cannot simplify content to a low enough level for children (De Belder and Moens, 2010).

Audience outline	*Datasets*	*Evaluation*	*Venue*
(1) ...such as children, people with low education, people who have reading disorders or dyslexia, and non-native speakers of the language.	NEWSELA WIKILARGE BIENDATA	Automatic	*ACL 2021*
(2) It provides reading assistance to children (Kajiwara et al., 2013), non-native speakers (Petersen and Ostendorf, 2007; Pellow and Eskenazi, 2014; Paetzold, 2016) and people with reading disabilities (Rello et al., 2013b)	NEWSELA	Automatic + 5 workers	*NAACL 2021*
(3) It can provide convenience for non-native speakers (Petersen and Ostendorf, 2007; Glavaš and Štajner, 2015; Paetzold and Specia, 2016c; Rello et al., 2013b), non-expert readers (Elhadad and Sutaria, 2007; Siddharthan and Katsos, 2010) and children (De Belder and Moens, 2010; Kajiwara et al., 2013)	D-WIKIPEDIA NEWSELA	Automatic + 3 workers	*EMNLP 2021*
(4) ...to children (De Belder and Moens, 2010; Kajiwara et al., 2013), people with language disabilities like aphasia (Carroll et al., 1998b, 1999b; Devlin and Unthank, 2006), dyslexia (Rello et al., 2013a,b), or autism (Evans et al., 2014); non-native (Petersen and Ostendorf, 2007; Paetzold, 2015; Paetzold and Specia, 2016b; Pellow and Eskenazi, 2014) English speakers, and people with low literacy skills or reading ages.	WIKISMALL WIKILARGE	Automatic	*BEA 2021*

Table 2: Examples of paper introductions outlining audiences benefiting from text simplification, alongside the evaluation techniques and venue, specific paper references are included in Appendix A.

Framing the benefit of text simplification as net positive for all groups can have consequences for the development of assistive technology, as merging the audiences serves to diminish the sensitive differences in needs for these groups. Even for specific audiences, such as children, there is a consensus that the homogeneous grouping of reading ability can have detrimental outcomes for learning (Schumm et al., 2000).

A further complication, is that the references commonly used in support of text simplification (for specific audiences) are often more nuanced than stated. For instance, the work of Rello et al. (2013a) is commonly cited as showing the benefit of text simplification for dyslexic readers. However, this paper demonstrates that the most effective strategy to help dyslexic readers with difficult words, is to provide a range of synonyms for the word, and not to simplify the original. Furthermore, the work of Carroll et al. (1998a) and Carroll et al. (1999a) is put forward as evidence for the utility of simplification for individuals with aphasia. However, both of these works outline the proposal for a simplification system targeted for aphasia and propose to evaluate the effectiveness of such a system in future work. A final example, used in support of text simplification for children is a paper by De Belder and Moens (2010). However, the paper finds that even using lexical and syntatic simplification, it was not possible to reduce the reading difficulty enough for children.

3.1.2 Datasets and Evaluation

Text simplification has many subtleties, as what would be a valid simplification for one reader may not be appropriate for another (Xu et al., 2015). For instance, it has been shown that the factors contributing to word complexity vary depending on the first language and proficiency level of a reader (Gooding et al., 2021b). The subjective nature of text simplification means that system evaluation is difficult. Furthermore, as there is not one 'ground truth' for simplification, the efficacy of automatic evaluation measures is limited. Prior work on the development and evaluation of simplification systems has given little consideration to the target reader population (Xu et al., 2015).

As exemplified in Table 2, current work on text simplification typically relies on automatic evaluation, with the occasional use of human evaluation.

When considering the approach to human evaluation, most work does not specify what "being simpler" entails, and trusts human judges to use their own understanding of the concept (Alva-Manchego et al., 2021). It is also currently not standard practice to include the demographic information of the workers. When using human judgements as a measure of simplification quality, it is important to include relevant information on the demographic background, so that valid conclusions can be drawn about which target population may benefit from the system. Additionally, the concept of what constitutes adequate simplification needs to be precise if the system is aimed for a specialised audience.

The datasets commonly used to train text simplification systems (i.e. Newsela and Simple Wikipedia) have drawbacks such as poor alignment, lack of simplicity and not being tailored for a specific audiences (Xu et al., 2015). In text simplification, it is important to discuss the limitations of the data so that the suitability of such systems for specialised groups is clearly recognised.

In summary, when claiming the benefits of text simplification for specific audiences, it is crucial that the needs of these groups are understood. This is especially the case when emphasising the benefit of such technology for disabled groups. The development of assistive technology is downstream from research, and therefore being clear about the suitability and limitations of the technology for differing audiences helps to avoid poorly suited assistive technology solutions being developed.

3.2 Meaning Distortion

There are multiple genres of text where access is highly important, such as healthcare information or political materials. The benefits of simplifying such content have been shown, for example simplifying text in health care improves understanding of information regardless of health literacy level (Kim and Kim, 2015). Furthermore, the complexity of language matters for voters' perceptions of political parties and their positions (Bischof and Senninger, 2018).

The benefit of text simplification in such cases is apparent, as is the need to ensure the meaning of such text is preserved and that no errors are introduced. A drawback to current automated text simplification systems is that the subtleties of meaning intended by the author may be diluted, if not lost altogether (Chandrasekar et al., 1996). For example, Shardlow and Nawaz (2019) found that fully automated approaches omitted 30% of critical information when used to simplify clinical texts. For these types of domains, instead of fully-automated approaches, interactive text simplification tools are better suited to generate more efficient and higher quality simplifications (Kloehn et al., 2018).

The link between factual correctness and natural language generation has been considered for multiple domains such as summarization (Cao et al., 2018), data to document generation (Wiseman et al., 2017) and dialog generation (Shuster et al., 2021). However, this is a relatively underexplored area for text simplification and is currently not incorporated into the evaluation of such systems.

Encouraging further discussion on this limitation of text simplification is necessary. Especially when we consider the downstream applications of assistive technology for critical consumer information.

3.3 Paternalism

There are choices made in the design characteristics of assistive technology that can affect the degree of independence, privacy and participation that are possible (Lenker et al., 2013). These decisions have real world impact for the users and thus warrant careful consideration.

The process of text simplification involves an understanding of *what* is difficult and *how* best to simplify it. There are two approaches when deciding *what* should be simplified. The first, involves including the reader in the loop – either implicitly or explicitly. Relying on user signal to identify areas for simplification has its own set of ethical concerns which are discussed in § 3.4. The second approach, is performing general level simplification with end-to-end systems. In fact, the majority of current work in text simplification is now data-driven and performs simplification in a 'black-box' fashion (Sikka and Mago, 2020). One of the concerns for such systems, is that they learn operations based on the simplification choices made in the data they are trained with. As outlined in Section 3.1.2, most of the data used to train text simplification systems is not audience specific (Xu et al., 2015).

Integrating general purpose simplification systems into assistive technologies has a range of potential problems. For instance, it raises the issue of "paternalism" which is the interference of a state or individual in relation to another person (Martin et al., 2007). The relationship between paternalism and assistive technology is widely acknowledged, as design decisions made on behalf of a user can be problematic if they override the autonomy of the individual (Martin et al., 2007, 2010). In the case of text simplification, not allowing the individual the choice of what they would want simplified restricts their autonomy.

Furthermore, assistive technologies should contribute to growth and independence for individuals. The goals of text simplification are to make textual information accessible to a range of different audiences. However, the question of whether such systems should support learning is rarely discussed. One concern with text simplification within assistive systems, is that it would prevent the exposure to new terms and concepts thereby encouraging learning stagnation.

In summary, the design decisions pertaining to what content is simplified have ethical implications for the user. Removing the individual from the decision process can reduce the person's autonomy, and not allowing exposure to new and unfamiliar terms limits learning opportunities, subsequently reducing the user's independence.

3.4 Privacy and Security

As outlined in Section 3.3, an effective approach for text simplification in assistive technology is to include the user in the decision of what is simplified. Prior research has shown that eye-tracking (Berzak et al., 2018) and scroll-based interactions (Gooding et al., 2021a) correlate with text understanding. As such, these implicit techniques can be used to gain an insight into what the reader is finding difficult. The reader can also be explicitly asked to select text that they would like to be simplified, for instance by selecting words that are difficult for them (Devlin and Unthank, 2006; Paetzold and Specia, 2016a).

Adaptive text simplification is advantageous and provides autonomy and learning opportunities for the user. However, the information about the areas a user finds difficult is highly sensitive, and there is a responsibility to ensure that such information is stored securely.

To protect the privacy of the user, the aim of the assistive technology and the way it is used by service providers or care organisations must be clear. Moreover, how personal data will be handled must be described explicitly in a privacy statement and communicated to the user (Martin et al., 2010).

The above is a clear example of how viewing text simplification through the paradigm of assistive technology yields more nuanced ethical considerations. We believe it would be beneficial to encourage the discourse on such aspects in the text simplification literature.

4 Going Forward

We suggest that papers focusing on general purpose text simplification should de-couple the motivations from specific audiences with disabilities. An example of a general purpose motivation by Nisioi et al. (2017) is as follows:

> *Automated text simplification (ATS) systems are meant to transform original texts into different (simpler) variants which would be understood by wider audiences and more successfully processed by various NLP tools.*

Alternatively, if discussing the different groups of users who may benefit from text simplification, being clear about the specific strategies that work for these audiences is critical. Additionally, it is worth acknowledging that when framing a system using a target demographic, it is appropriate that the system is tested with that target group. For human evaluation generally, it is highly beneficial to report the demographic statistics, as this allows an insight into which types of audiences the system may work well for.

Finally, it is important to be forthright about the current limitations of both the data and evaluation techniques used in automatic text simplification. Whilst great improvements are being made in this area, these systems are still far from perfect and this needs to be taken into account when judging the suitability of systems for assistive technology.

5 Conclusion

Assistive technologies can dramatically affect the lives of those who rely on them, and it is important to understand the potential ethical concerns – especially as such technologies can impact vulnerable populations. In this paper, we discuss a set of potential issues that arise from the embedding of text simplification within assistive technologies.

Our aim in this work is to encourage further discussion on how the design decisions of text simplification algorithms can have the potential to impact future users of assistive technology.

References

Fernando Alva-Manchego, Carolina Scarton, and Lucia Specia. 2021. The (un) suitability of automatic evaluation metrics for text simplification. *Computational Linguistics*, 47(4):861–889.

Yevgeni Berzak, Boris Katz, and Roger Levy. 2018. Assessing language proficiency from eye movements in reading. In *Proceedings of the 2018 Conference of the North American Chapter of the Association for Computational Linguistics: Human Language Technologies, Volume 1 (Long Papers)*, pages 1986–1996, New Orleans, Louisiana. Association for Computational Linguistics.

Daniel Bischof and Roman Senninger. 2018. Simple politics for the people? complexity in campaign messages and political knowledge. *European Journal of Political Research*, 57(2):473–495.

Johan Borg, Stig Larsson, and Per-Olof Östergren. 2011. The right to assistive technology: For whom, for what, and by whom? *Disability & Society*, 26(2):151–167.

Necati Cihan Camgoz, Simon Hadfield, Oscar Koller, Hermann Ney, and Richard Bowden. 2018. Neural sign language translation. In *Proceedings of the IEEE conference on computer vision and pattern recognition*, pages 7784–7793.

Yvonne Canning, John Tait, Jackie Archibald, and Ros Crawley. 2000. Cohesive generation of syntactically simplified newspaper text. In *Proceedings of the Third International Workshop on Text, Speech and Dialogue (TDS '00)*, pages 145–150.

Ziqiang Cao, Furu Wei, Wenjie Li, and Sujian Li. 2018. Faithful to the original: Fact aware neural abstractive summarization. In *thirty-second AAAI conference on artificial intelligence*.

John Carroll, Gido Minnen, Yvonne Canning, Siobhan Devlin, and John Tait. 1998a. Practical simplification of English newspaper text to assist aphasic readers. In *Proceedings of AAAI Workshop on Integrating AI and Assistive Technology*, pages 7–10.

John Carroll, Guido Minnen, Yvonne Canning, Siobhan Devlin, and John Tait. 1998b. Practical simplification of english newspaper text to assist aphasic readers. In *Proceedings of the AAAI-98 Workshop on Integrating Artificial Intelligence and Assistive Technology*, pages 7–10. Citeseer.

John Carroll, Guido Minnen, Darren Pearce, Yvonne Canning, Siobhan Devlin, and John Tait. 1999a. Simplifying Text for Language-Impaired Readers. In *Proceedings of the 9th Conference of the European Chapter of the ACL (EACL'99)*, pages 269–270, Bergen, Norway.

John A Carroll, Guido Minnen, Darren Pearce, Yvonne Canning, Siobhan Devlin, and John Tait. 1999b. Simplifying text for language-impaired readers. In *Ninth Conference of the European Chapter of the Association for Computational Linguistics*, pages 269–270.

Raman Chandrasekar, Christine Doran, and Srinivas Bangalore. 1996. Motivations and methods for text simplification. In *COLING 1996 Volume 2: The 16th International Conference on Computational Linguistics*.

William Coster and David Kauchak. 2011. Learning to Simplify Sentences Using Wikipedia. In *Proceedings of the Workshop on Monolingual Text-To-Text Generation*, pages 1–9.

Jan De Belder and Marie-Francine Moens. 2010. Text simplification for children. In *Proceedings of the SIGIR workshop on accessible search systems*, pages 19–26. ACM.

Siobhan Devlin and Gary Unthank. 2006. Helping aphasic people process online information. In *Proceedings of the 8th international ACM SIGACCESS conference on Computers and accessibility*, pages 225–226.

Yue Dong, Zichao Li, Mehdi Rezagholizadeh, and Jackie Chi Kit Cheung. 2019. EditNTS: An neural programmer-interpreter model for sentence simplification through explicit editing. In *Proceedings of the 57th Annual Meeting of the Association for Computational Linguistics*, pages 3393–3402, Florence, Italy. Association for Computational Linguistics.

Noemie Elhadad and Komal Sutaria. 2007. Mining a lexicon of technical terms and lay equivalents. In *Biological, translational, and clinical language processing*, pages 49–56.

Richard Evans, Constantin Orasan, and Iustin Dornescu. 2014. An evaluation of syntactic simplification rules for people with autism. Association for Computational Linguistics.

Cristina Garbacea, Mengtian Guo, Samuel Carton, and Qiaozhu Mei. 2021. Explainable prediction of text complexity: The missing preliminaries for text simplification. In *Proceedings of the 59th Annual Meeting of the Association for Computational Linguistics and the 11th International Joint Conference on Natural Language Processing (Volume 1: Long Papers)*, pages 1086–1097, Online. Association for Computational Linguistics.

Goran Glavaš and Sanja Štajner. 2015. Simplifying lexical simplification: do we need simplified corpora? In *Proceedings of the 53rd Annual Meeting of the Association for Computational Linguistics and the 7th International Joint Conference on Natural Language Processing (Volume 2: Short Papers)*, volume 2, pages 63–68.

Sian Gooding, Yevgeni Berzak, Tony Mak, and Matt Sharifi. 2021a. Predicting text readability from scrolling interactions. In *Proceedings of the 25th Conference on Computational Natural Language Learning*, pages 380–390, Online. Association for Computational Linguistics.

Sian Gooding and Ekaterina Kochmar. 2019. Recursive context-aware lexical simplification. In *Proceedings of the 2019 Conference on Empirical Methods in Natural Language Processing and the 9th International Joint Conference on Natural Language Processing (EMNLP-IJCNLP)*, pages 4853–4863, Hong Kong, China. Association for Computational Linguistics.

Sian Gooding, Ekaterina Kochmar, Seid Muhie Yimam, and Chris Biemann. 2021b. Word complexity is in the eye of the beholder. In *Proceedings of the 2021 Conference of the North American Chapter of the Association for Computational Linguistics: Human Language Technologies*, pages 4439–4449, Online. Association for Computational Linguistics.

Tomoyuki Kajiwara, Hiroshi Matsumoto, and Kazuhide Yamamoto. 2013. Selecting proper lexical paraphrase for children. In *Proceedings of the 25th Conference on Computational Linguistics and Speech Processing (ROCLING 2013)*, pages 59–73.

David Kauchak. 2013. Improving Text Simplification Language Modeling Using Unsimplified Text Data. In *Proceedings of the 51st Annual Meeting of the Association for Computational Linguistics (Volume 1: Long Papers)*, pages 1537–1546.

Eun Jin Kim and Su Hyun Kim. 2015. Simplification improves understanding of informed consent information in clinical trials regardless of health literacy level. *Clinical Trials*, 12(3):232–236.

Nicholas Kloehn, Gondy Leroy, David Kauchak, Yang Gu, Sonia Colina, Nicole P Yuan, Debra Revere, et al. 2018. Improving consumer understanding of medical text: Development and validation of a new subsimplify algorithm to automatically generate term explanations in english and spanish. *Journal of medical Internet research*, 20(8):e10779.

James A Lenker, Frances Harris, Mary Taugher, and Roger O Smith. 2013. Consumer perspectives on assistive technology outcomes. *Disability and Rehabilitation: Assistive Technology*, 8(5):373–380.

Mounica Maddela, Fernando Alva-Manchego, and Wei Xu. 2021. Controllable text simplification with explicit paraphrasing. In *Proceedings of the 2021 Conference of the North American Chapter of the Association for Computational Linguistics: Human Language Technologies*, pages 3536–3553, Online. Association for Computational Linguistics.

Suzanne Martin, Johan E Bengtsson, and Rose-Marie Dröes. 2010. Assistive technologies and issues relating to privacy, ethics and security. In *Supporting people with dementia using pervasive health technologies*, pages 63–76. Springer.

Suzanne Martin, Colm Cunningham, and Chris Nugent. 2007. Ethical considerations for integrating technology. *Alzheimer's Care Today*, 8(3):251–258.

Alistair R Niemeijer, Brenda JM Frederiks, Ingrid I Riphagen, Johan Legemaate, Jan A Eefsting, and Cees MPM Hertogh. 2010. Ethical and practical concerns of surveillance technologies in residential care for people with dementia or intellectual disabilities: an overview of the literature. *International Psychogeriatrics*, 22(7):1129–1142.

Sergiu Nisioi, Sanja Štajner, Simone Paolo Ponzetto, and Liviu P Dinu. 2017. Exploring neural text simplification models. In *Proceedings of the 55th Annual Meeting of the Association for Computational Linguistics (Volume 2: Short Papers)*, pages 85–91.

Kostiantyn Omelianchuk, Vipul Raheja, and Oleksandr Skurzhanskyi. 2021. Text Simplification by Tagging. In *Proceedings of the 16th Workshop on Innovative Use of NLP for Building Educational Applications*, pages 11–25, Online. Association for Computational Linguistics.

Gustavo Paetzold. 2015. Reliable lexical simplification for non-native speakers. In *Proceedings of the 2015 Conference of the North American Chapter of the Association for Computational Linguistics: Student Research Workshop*, pages 9–16.

Gustavo Paetzold and Lucia Specia. 2016a. Anita: An intelligent text adaptation tool. In *Proceedings of COLING 2016, the 26th International Conference on Computational Linguistics: System Demonstrations*, pages 79–83.

Gustavo Paetzold and Lucia Specia. 2016b. Understanding the lexical simplification needs of non-native speakers of english. In *Proceedings of COLING 2016, the 26th International Conference on Computational Linguistics: Technical Papers*, pages 717–727.

Gustavo Paetzold and Lucia Specia. 2016c. Unsupervised lexical simplification for non-native speakers. In *Proceedings of the AAAI Conference on Artificial Intelligence*, volume 30.

Gustavo H Paetzold and Lucia Specia. 2017. A survey on lexical simplification. *Journal of Artificial Intelligence Research*, 60:549–593.

Gustavo Henrique Paetzold. 2016. *Lexical Simplification for Non-Native English Speakers*. Ph.D. thesis, University of Sheffield.

David Pellow and Maxine Eskenazi. 2014. An open corpus of everyday documents for simplification tasks. In *Proceedings of the 3rd Workshop on Predicting and Improving Text Readability for Target Reader Populations (PITR)*, pages 84–93.

Sarah E Petersen and Mari Ostendorf. 2007. Text simplification for language learners: a corpus analysis. In *Workshop on speech and language technology in education*. Citeseer.

Karen Preston. 2003. Assistive technologies: Principles and practice. *Rehabilitation Nursing*, 28(2):64.

Luz Rello, Ricardo Baeza-Yates, Stefan Bott, and Horacio Saggion. 2013a. Simplify or help? text simplification strategies for people with dyslexia. In *Proceedings of the 10th International Cross-Disciplinary Conference on Web Accessibility*, pages 1–10.

Luz Rello, Ricardo Baeza-Yates, and Horacio Saggion. 2013b. The impact of lexical simplification by verbal paraphrases for people with and without dyslexia. In *International Conference on Intelligent Text Processing and Computational Linguistics*, pages 501–512. Springer.

Jeanne Shay Schumm, Sally W Moody, and Sharon Vaughn. 2000. Grouping for reading instruction: Does one size fit all? *Journal of learning disabilities*, 33(5):477–488.

Matthew Shardlow and Raheel Nawaz. 2019. Neural text simplification of clinical letters with a domain specific phrase table.

Kurt Shuster, Spencer Poff, Moya Chen, Douwe Kiela, and Jason Weston. 2021. Retrieval augmentation reduces hallucination in conversation. In *Findings of the Association for Computational Linguistics: EMNLP 2021*, pages 3784–3803, Punta Cana, Dominican Republic. Association for Computational Linguistics.

Advaith Siddharthan. 2006a. Syntactic simplification and text cohesion. *Research on Language and Computation*, 4(1):77–109.

Advaith Siddharthan. 2006b. Syntactic Simplification and Text Cohesion. *Research on Language and Computation*, 4:77–109.

Advaith Siddharthan. 2014. A survey of research on text simplification. *ITL-International Journal of Applied Linguistics*, 165(2):259–298.

Advaith Siddharthan and Napoleon Katsos. 2010. Reformulating discourse connectives for non-expert readers. In *Human Language Technologies: The 2010 Annual Conference of the North American Chapter of the Association for Computational Linguistics*, pages 1002–1010.

Punardeep Sikka and Vijay Mago. 2020. A survey on text simplification. *arXiv preprint arXiv:2008.08612*.

R Sriranjani, Srinivasan Umesh, and M Ramasubba Reddy. 2015. Pronunciation adaptation for disordered speech recognition using state-specific vectors of phone-cluster adaptive training. In *Proceedings of SLPAT 2015: 6th Workshop on Speech and Language Processing for Assistive Technologies*, pages 72–78.

Renliang Sun, Hanqi Jin, and Xiaojun Wan. 2021. Document-level text simplification: Dataset, criteria and baseline. In *Proceedings of the 2021 Conference on Empirical Methods in Natural Language Processing*, pages 7997–8013, Online and Punta Cana, Dominican Republic. Association for Computational Linguistics.

Christophe Veaux, Junichi Yamagishi, and Simon King. 2013. Towards personalised synthesised voices for individuals with vocal disabilities: Voice banking and reconstruction. In *Proceedings of the Fourth Workshop on Speech and Language Processing for Assistive Technologies*, pages 107–111.

Sam Wiseman, Stuart Shieber, and Alexander Rush. 2017. Challenges in data-to-document generation. In *Proceedings of the 2017 Conference on Empirical Methods in Natural Language Processing*, pages 2253–2263, Copenhagen, Denmark. Association for Computational Linguistics.

Sander Wubben, Antal Van Den Bosch, and Emiel Krahmer. 2012. Sentence simplification by monolingual machine translation. In *Proceedings of the 50th Annual Meeting of the Association for Computational Linguistics: Long Papers-Volume 1*, pages 1015–1024. Association for Computational Linguistics.

Wei Xu, Chris Callison-Burch, and Courtney Napoles. 2015. Problems in Current Text Simplification Research: New Data Can Help. *Transactions of the Association for Computational Linguistics (TACL)*, 3:283–297.

Dolly N Young. 1999. Linguistic simplification of sl reading material: Effective instructional practice? *The Modern Language Journal*, 83(3):350–366.

Xingxing Zhang and Mirella Lapata. 2017. Sentence Simplification with Deep Reinforcement Learning. In *Proceedings of the 2017 Conference on Empirical Methods in Natural Language Processing*, pages 584–594.

Zhemin Zhu, Delphine Bernhard, and Iryna Gurevych. 2010. A Monolingual Tree-based Translation Model for Sentence Simplification. In *Proceedings of the 23rd International Conference on Computational Linguistics (Coling 2010)*, pages 1353–1361.

A Appendix

Paper references from Table 2:

1. Explainable Prediction of Text Complexity: The Missing Preliminaries for Text Simplification by Garbacea et al. (2021)

2. by Controllable Text Simplification with Explicit Paraphrasing by Maddela et al. (2021)

3. Document-Level Text Simplification: Dataset, Criteria and Baseline by Sun et al. (2021)

4. Text Simplification by Tagging by Omelianchuk et al. (2021)

Applying the Stereotype Content Model to assess disability bias in popular pre-trained NLP models underlying AI-based assistive technologies

Brienna Herold and **James Waller** and **Raja S. Kushalnagar**
Gallaudet University,
800 Florida Ave NE, Washington, DC 20002 USA
brienna.herold@gmail.com, james.waller@gallaudet.edu, raja.kushalnagar@gallaudet.edu

Abstract

Stereotypes are a positive or negative, generalized, and often widely shared belief about the attributes of certain groups of people, such as people with sensory disabilities. If stereotypes manifest in assistive technologies used by deaf or blind people, they can harm the user in a number of ways—especially considering the vulnerable nature of the target population. AI models underlying assistive technologies have been shown to contain biased stereotypes, including racial, gender, and disability biases. We build on this work to present a psychology-based stereotype assessment of the representation of disability, deafness, and blindness in BERT using the Stereotype Content Model. We show that BERT contains disability bias, and that this bias differs along established stereotype dimensions.

1 Introduction

Pre-trained natural language processing (NLP) models are becoming more commonly deployed in pipelines for consumer tools, including those that fall under the umbrella of assistive technologies. Models such as BERT are used in tools that utilize automatic text simplification (ATS) for reading assistance (Lauscher et al., 2020), where complex words get replaced with simpler alternatives. BERT is also used in natural language understanding tools such as automatic speech recognition (Chuang et al., 2020).

In addition to a continuing increase in the use cases and complexity of AI-based assistive technologies, there is also growing interest in using them. Alonzo et al. (2020) found that the deaf community expressed strong interest in ATS-based reading assistance tools. To achieve fair and inclusive experiences for deaf and blind people, it is important to understand how they may be represented by the models underlying the assistive technologies that are designed for them (Kafle et al., 2019).

If an AI-based consumer tool perpetuates existing biases and stereotypes in society, it can inadvertently cause and reinforce structural stigma, or "societal level conditions, cultural norms, and institutional policies that constrain the opportunities, resources, and well-being of the stigmatized" (Hatzenbuehler, 2016). The bias against deafness—or audism—is prevalent in both mainstream society (Humphries, 1977) and in the deaf community (Gertz, 2003). Audism has been linked to discrimination in multiple real-world scenarios, including the job application process (Task Force Members and Contributors, 2012). In Szymanski (2010), 100% of highly qualified psychology internship applications that mentioned deafness were rejected, whereas 100% of those that didn't mention deafness were invited for an interview.

Causing or reinforcing structural stigma can lead to allocational and representational harms (Blodgett et al., 2020). Allocational harms arise if assistive technologies distribute resources or opportunities unfairly to disabled people. With representational harms, if assistive technologies represent these people unfairly, disabled people may experience alienation, decreased quality of service, stereotypes, denigration and stigmatization, erasure, and/or decreased public participation.

Despite recent ballooning of research in NLP fairness (Sheng et al., 2020; Blodgett, 2021), there has been little investigation into how AI models represent disabled people, who comprise at least 12.5% of the global population (WHO, 2021). There has been even less of a focus on how people with sensory disabilities are represented in NLP models. Hutchinson et al. (2020) provided preliminary evidence that disability-mentioning text may be accidentally flagged as toxic. Hassan et al. (2021) detected signs of disability bias in BERT using sentiment analysis, and they investigated how this bias might shift when applying an intersectional lens to the analysis.

Ninth Workshop on Speech and Language Processing for Assistive Technologies (SLPAT-2022), pages 58 - 65
May 27, 2022

To further investigate sensory disability bias in NLP models, we build upon prior work in association bias in BERT. Our contributions include adapting Kurita et al. (2019)'s sentence templates to examine associations between disability qualifiers and stereotype traits, drawing from the Stereotype Content Model (SCM), an established approach in social psychology to defining stereotyped bias (Fiske et al., 2002).

Specifically, we answer these research questions:

- **RQ1**. In BERT, is there evidence of bias in how the model perceives disability, compared to ability?
- **RQ2**. Do BERT's representations of ability and disability differ across various stereotype dimensions?

2 Related Work

We review previous work in examining stereotypes in NLP models, and then we briefly describe the SCM and its relevance to measuring bias.

2.1 Stereotypes in NLP models

Bolukbasi et al. (2016) first observed that gender stereotypes are present in static word embeddings (e.g. word2vec and GloVe) using subspace analysis. Caliskan et al. (2017) found that word embeddings capture a spectrum of implicit biases, using lexicons developed for the Implicit Association Test, or the IAT (Greenwald et al., 1998), and calculated associations within static word embeddings. Kurita et al. (2019) extended this approach to work with contextualized embedding models such as BERT.

However, using word lists pulled from the IAT is limiting when it comes to assessing disability bias, since the relevant tests incorporate images instead of words. For this reason, there has been more work in downstream tasks such as sentiment analysis and topic modelling (Hutchinson et al., 2020; Hassan et al., 2021), and less in direct association analysis.

2.2 Stereotype Content Model (SCM)

Stereotypes have been studied in social psychology for decades (Asch, 1946; Greenwald et al., 1998; Fiske et al., 2007). To concisely summarize the current knowledge about stereotypes, Fiske et al. (2002) proposed the SCM, which postulates that stereotypes can be aligned along two dimensions: competence and warmth. When we meet someone new, our first psychological response is to subconsciously evaluate whether they are a friend or a foe. This is a judgement along the warmth dimension. Immediately after we make this evaluation, we go on to evaluate how well they may be able to act in accordance to our perception of their warmth. Abele et al. (2016); Nicolas et al. (2021) suggested that these dimensions can be further split into two subdimensions. Warmth is comprised of Morality and Sociability, and competence is comprised of Agency and Ability.

Researchers working under the SCM framework also propose a causal link between stereotypes and structural stigma (Fiske et al., 2007). People perceived as warm and competent evoke feelings of pride and admiration, whereas people perceived as cold and incompetent evoke feelings of disgust and contempt. Ambivalent perceptions involving warmth and incompetence typically elicit pity and sympathy. Coldness and competence evokes envy and jealousy. These biases, whether explicit or implicit, can lead to harms if they are perpetuated in AI-based assistive technologies.

To the best of our knowledge, Fraser et al. (2021) is the only work to date that has applied the SCM to analyze stereotypes in text. The SCM has not yet been used to investigate stereotypes in NLP models.

3 Methods

Following Kurita et al. (2019) and Bartl et al. (2020), we measured association bias in BERT using a fill-in-the-blank task, and synthetic, semantically bleached sentence templates. Our goal was to directly examine representations in the model, without potential interference from unexpected context or downstream input, which may occur when using natural sentence templates or with tasks such as sentiment analysis and topic modelling.

3.1 Data

Table 1 displays the targets, stereotype attribute dimensions, and sentence templates used in our study. For the targets, we used three abled/disabled antonym pairs to represent the concepts of ability and disability for general ability, deafness, and blindness. We recognize that some words such as "hearing" may not be commonly used in mainstream society, and in turn may not appear often as a person-describing qualifier in the Wikipedia and Books Corpus, which BERT was pre-trained on.

Targets	
disabled	abled
deaf	hearing
blind	sighted

Stereotype Dimension	Subdimension	Attributes
Warmth	Sociable	155
	Unsociable	156
	Moral	159
	Immoral	334
Competence	Able	153
	Unable	127
	Independent	156
	Dependent	109

	Templates
1	A `[TARGET]` person is `[ATTRIBUTE]`.
2	`[TARGET]` people are `[ATTRIBUTE]`.
3	A person who is `[TARGET]` is `[ATTRIBUTE]`.
4	People who are `[TARGET]` are `[ATTRIBUTE]`.

Table 1: Targets, stereotype attribute dimensions, and semantically bleached templates. The syntactic structure of templates 1 and 2 is typical of identity-first language, whereas templates 3 and 4 use person-first language.

However this word represents how the members of the deaf community describe those who hear. It is important to explore how a model may represent a word that has different usage in certain communities, if the model is used in end-applications by those communities.

Taking inspiration from Fraser et al. (2021), we constructed the stereotype subdimensions using the extended lexicon created by Nicolas et al. (2021), with the four subdimensions of Morality, Sociability, Agency, and Ability. In this lexicon, words are annotated with either +1 or -1 to indicate a positive or negative association with the given subdimension. We removed words that were not labelled with either valence value. We represent each valence pole of these subdimensions as their own subdimension, e.g. words with a negative association to Morality represent the Immoral subdimension. We expect these 8 subdimensions to provide a more granular understanding of stereotyped representations in BERT.

We used four semantically bleached sentence templates, which are shown in Table 1. We adapted them from Kurita et al. (2019) and Hutchinson et al. (2020). The first two templates use identity-first language, in which `[TARGET]` precedes "person." Despite removing context, the syntactic structure of the sentence itself is known to carry cultural connotations (Beukeboom and Burgers, 2019; Shakespeare, 2016). Members of the deaf community often prefer to use identity-first language, whereas the person-first language is usually found in a medical lens. To get a general picture of associations, we also include two templates that use person-first language, in which `[TARGET]` follows "person."

We removed words that would not fit the grammar of our selected templates. We kept adjectives, as identified by WordNet part-of-speech labelling. This leaves 1,256 unique words in this lexicon. Most belong to one subdimension, while 87 words belong to two subdimensions (e.g. "negligent" belongs to both the Immoral and Unable subdimensions), and 3 words belong to three subdimensions (e.g., "ingenuous" belongs to the Sociable, Immoral, and Unable subdimensions).

To further reduce possible causes of variation, we also removed all multi-word attributes. Although we are able to mask a couple of words in a sentence when feeding it to BERT, as done in Bartl et al. (2020), it is not possible to predict the probability of a multi-word phrase, only a single subtoken. Most of our targets are whole tokens, except for "abled," which is a multi-token word: "able" + "ed". We multiplied the probabilities for the subtokens that make up this word, since it is implicit that these subtokens are associated.

The final dataset consisted of 30,144 combinations of targets, attributes, and templates.

3.2 Measuring Bias in BERT

We used the `PyTorch` implementation of the `transformers` library from HuggingFace, a widely used hub for the distribution of pre-trained Transformer models (Wolf et al., 2020). We downloaded `bert-base-uncased`, the most popular version of BERT according to download count, along with a language modeling head on top and its tokenizer.

Below we outline our methodology to measure bias in BERT, which we adapted from Kurita et al. (2019).

1. Prepare semantically bleached template sentences. For example,

   A [TARGET] person is [ATTRIBUTE].

2. For each combination of target, attribute, and template,

   (a) Fill in the template.
   "A deaf person is eligible."

   (b) Mask the target.
   "A [MASK] person is eligible."

   (c) Compute the target's probability, given the context provided by the attribute.

   $p_x = P(\text{[MASK]} = \text{"deaf"} \mid \text{sentence})$

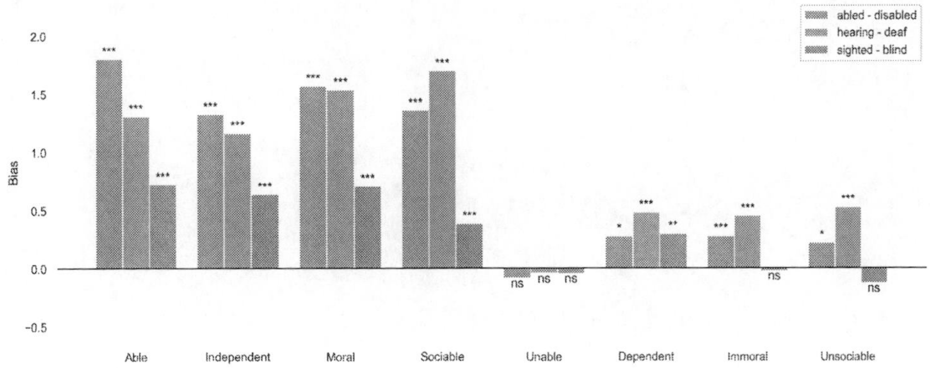

Figure 1: Bias scores for pairs of targets, when the target is predicted in the presence of the attribute. Each bias score is annotated with statistical significance where $n.s.$ means the bias is not significant at $p > 0.05$, $*$ is $p \leq 0.05$, $**$ means $p \leq 0.01$, and $***$ is highly significant at $p \leq 0.001$. The further the score gets from zero, the more unequal the representations of ability and disability. Scores above zero indicate that BERT more closely associates the abled target with the corresponding stereotype subdimension, whereas scores below zero indicate a bias where the model prefers the disabled target more, given the stereotype context. These results show evidence of significant, nuanced bias in how BERT represents disability, compared to ability.

(d) Mask both the target and attribute.
"A [MASK] person is [MASK]."

(e) Compute the target's prior probability, given no context.

$$p_{prior} = P(\text{[MASK]}=\text{"deaf"} \mid masked\_sentence)$$

(f) Compute the association (a) between the target (x) and attribute (m).

$$a_{x,m} = \log\left(\frac{P_x}{P_{prior}}\right)$$

(g) Compute the mean association score (A) between the target (x) and the attribute subdimension (M).

$$A_{x,M} = mean_{m \in M}\, a_{x,m}$$

(h) Compute the bias score for the attribute subdimension (M) as the difference between the mean association scores for two targets.

$$bias_M = A_{y,M} - A_{x,M}$$

If the association is negative, this means that the target's probability is lower than its prior probability. In other words, the attribute's context *decreased* the probability that BERT predicts the target. Likewise, if the association is positive, the context *increased* the target's probability of being predicted.

In all bias calculations, the minuend is the abled target's association score, and the subtrahend is the disabled target's association score. Thus, if the bias is positive, the association between the abled target and the attribute subdimension is stronger. If the bias is negative, the disabled target is more strongly associated to the attribute subdimension. If the bias is zero, there is no difference in the probability of predicting either target, given the context.

We measured statistical significance via a paired-attribute permutation test over $A_{y,M}$ and $A_{x,M}$.

We also performed the inverse analysis, where we explored the representation of stereotype content given the presence of ability or disability. To carry out this analysis, we essentially treated attributes as targets, meaning that we masked the attribute and computed its probability, given the context provided by the target. Aside from this swap, the overall methodology remains the same.

4 Results and Discussion

Figure 1 displays the bias score between each pair of targets (abled/disabled antonyms, e.g. "hearing" and "deaf") for each stereotype subdimension in the SCM. Here we can see certain patterns in how disability is represented in BERT, compared to ability.

The first takeaway from this figure is that there is a bias, or a difference, in the representations, confirming **RQ1**. The bias is significant at varying levels across all subdimensions except the Unable subdimension. Correlation in language usage may have contributed to the lack of bias in the Unable subdimension. Mentions of disability are often accompanied by words referring to ability, and often in a negative, medical context where disability is

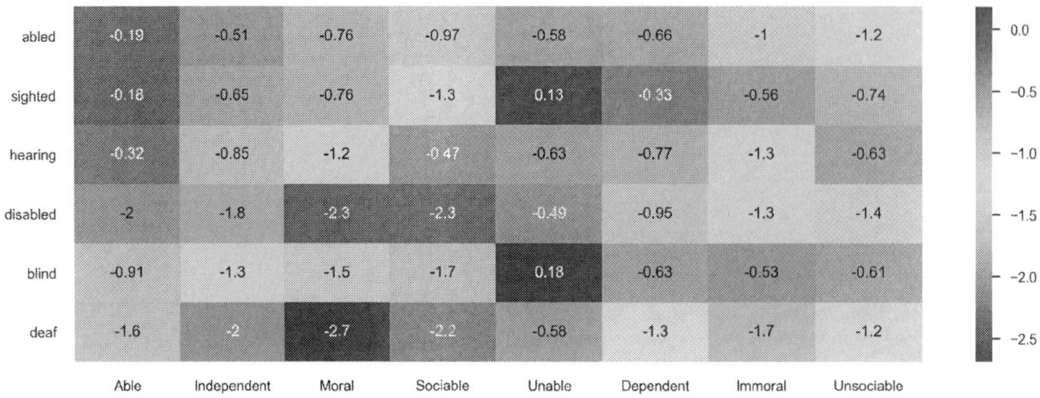

Figure 2: Mean association scores for each combination of target and stereotype subdimension. The further the score is from zero, the stronger the association is in BERT. If the score is above zero, this means that BERT positively associates the target with the stereotype subdimension. Conversely, if the score is below zero, BERT negatively associates the target with the stereotype subdimension. These results reveal patterns in how BERT's representations of ability and disability align to known stereotype subdimensions.

framed as a problem on the body, rather than on society (Shakespeare, 2016).

The second takeaway is that BERT is generally more likely to associate the abled target to all stereotype subdimensions, except the Unable subdimension for all three pairs of targets, and the Immoral and Unsociable subdimensions for blindness. This partiality toward ability may been caused by higher frequencies of abled targets in the training data (Schick and Schütze, 2020). People with disabilities are an underrepresented population and are thus mentioned less in mainstream text; there is an ongoing project to improve one of the training datasets to create more text related to disability (Wikipedia contributors, 2022). It is also less common to use an abled target to describe a person without a disability (Beukeboom and Burgers, 2019), and this in addition to these words' increased frequency may have led BERT to "understand" them better but in different contexts.

The third takeaway is that the bias is stronger if the sentence includes a positive warmth (Moral, Sociable) or competence (Able, Independent) context, presenting a high-level insight into **RQ2**. Given a positive stereotype context, BERT is more likely to predict the abled target than the disabled target in the fill-in-the-blank task. In other words, BERT is less likely to associate disability to warmth and competence. This bias is significant for ability, deafness, and blindness at $p \leq 0.001$.

On the other hand (or the other side of the figure), the bias between abled/disabled antonym target pairs is weaker if the sentence includes a negative warmth (Immoral, Unsociable) or competence (Dependent) context. This smaller difference in representation is still significant for deafness at $p \leq 0.001$, significant for general ability at varying levels, and significant for blindness with only the Dependent subdimension at $p \leq 0.01$.

To investigate **RQ2** in more depth, we show in Figure 2 the mean association scores for each combination of target (an abled or disabled antonym) and stereotype subdimension. This figure reveals more nuanced patterns in BERT's representation of disability and how this representation aligns to stereotype subdimensions from the SCM.

One pattern that stands out is that almost all of the mean association scores are negative, regardless of target or subdimension. A negative association score indicates that BERT is less likely to predict the target given the stereotype content *and* the syntactic structure of the sentence template. These negative association scores provide further support for BERT having limited knowledge about abled targets' range of usage, and/or the under-representation of disabled targets in the model.

Figure 2 also sheds additional light on the weaker bias shown in Figure 1 for negative subdimensions. Although BERT may have an overall preference for abled targets, the disabled targets' associations to these negative subdimensions are strong enough to appear nearly on par with the abled targets' associations to the same subdimen-

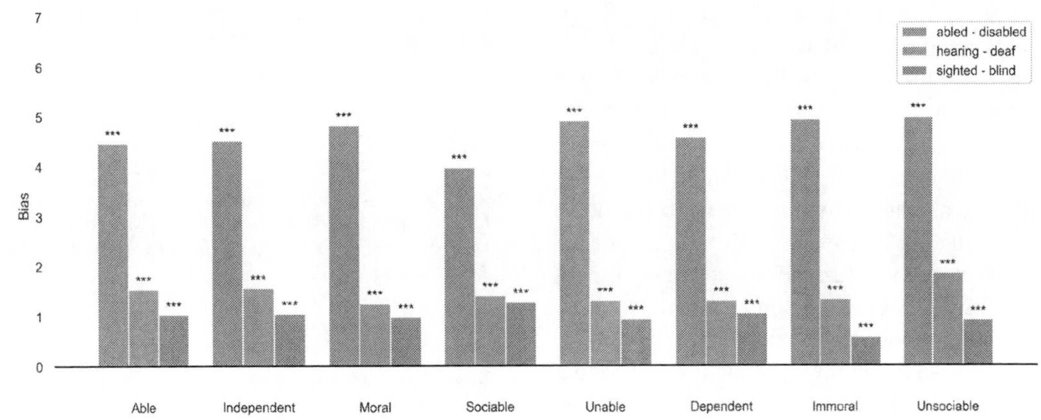

Figure 3: Bias scores for pairs of targets, when the attribute is predicted in the presence of the target. For interpretation details, please refer to Figure 1. These results show evidence that BERT is less likely to predict any attribute given an accompanying disability context. BERT contains significantly stronger associations between all stereotype attribute subdimensions and the abled target.

sions.

A third takeaway from Figure 2 is that disabled targets are less associated with Able, Independent, Moral, and Sociable contexts, compared to all other associations. This is especially pronounced with "disabled" and "deaf".

In Figure 4, the bias scores from the inverse analysis present evidence that predicting different attributes given the same target do not lead to different biases. Different stereotype subdimensions are not any closely combined with different targets, when the target context is already present in the sentence. However, BERT shows a general preference for predicting any attribute in the presence of abled targets, since the bias scores are all significantly positive, especially for ability.

We want to note that, despite semantic bleaching, syntactic differences in the sentence templates affected the strength of the association scores, but not the patterns. When using identity-first templates to predict a target given stereotype content, BERT more strongly associated "abled" and "hearing" to all subdimensions, whereas "sighted", "disabled", "blind", and "deaf" had stronger associations to all attribute subdimensions using person-first templates.

This is interesting, because identity-first and person-first language are known to carry cultural connotations. Furthermore, some common identity-first disability qualifiers, such as "disabled" and "deaf", and "blind" are used in contexts outside of social identity categories, e.g. as metaphors: "deaf as a post," "deaf and blind to [insert situation]". This may have impacted how they were understood by the model, and subsequently how they are predicted in identity-first or person-first language contexts.

5 Conclusions and Future Work

Regardless of how biases manifest, the first step toward ensuring harmless use of AI-based assistive technologies is to understand how target users are represented in the underlying models. By applying the Stereotype Content Model to evaluate representational differences, we present evidence of disability association bias in a popular pre-trained NLP model that is used in state-of-the-art AI-based assistive technologies such as text simplification and speech recognition.

We also present a breakdown of this bias along stereotype dimensions, which uncovers nuanced patterns in undesirable associations between disability and stereotypes, the most notable being that disabled people are significantly less likely to be associated to warmth and competence. Our results emphasize the need to work toward more fair and inclusive assistive technologies, especially since disabled people are the target population for these tools.

There are a number of limitations with our study. First, we explored these associations through a broad lens, looking at only ability versus disability. It is important to recognize that disability is not a siloed, unitary concept (Peña et al., 2016). Future work should investigate the associations through an intersectional lens (Crenshaw, 1989), to better understand how disability bias is affected by the interconnected nature of social categorizations.

A second limitation of our study is our usage of sentence templates. Despite attempts to semantically strip a sentence to provide a neutral context, BERT still draws on the syntactic structure of the sentence itself to help make its predictions (Devlin et al., 2019). We took this into consideration by varying the structure. However, we observed that association strengths appear to be influenced to a degree by syntactic differences. Future work can investigate stabilizing the bias evaluation metrics by including more templates and a wider range of sentence structure, or randomly sampling a natural sentence dataset. It would also be interesting to further differentiate between identity-first and person-first language, as well as to explore question-answering templates.

Third, we examined a limited number of targets and only in one model, BERT. Future work can extend our approach to evaluate additional disabled targets in additional models, such as GPT-2 (Radford et al., 2018) and GPT-3 (Radford et al., 2019), to get a fuller picture of disability representation in a wider range of popular pre-trained NLP models underlying AI-based assistive technologies.

Future work can also draw on debiasing approaches to mitigate bias in these models. We want to note that it is important in this work to also take into consideration the specific model deployment context, because enforcing fairness in an inappropriate context can result in the unintended erasure of a marginalized population (Blodgett, 2021). We provided an array of possible causes of the stereotype patterns that we observed, and these can be avenues for exploring debiasing solutions.

References

Andrea E. Abele, Nicole Hauke, Kim Peters, Eva Louvet, Aleksandra Szymkow, and Yanping Duan. 2016. Facets of the Fundamental Content Dimensions: Agency with Competence and Assertiveness—Communion with Warmth and Morality. *Frontiers in Psychology*, 7.

Oliver Alonzo, Lisa Elliot, Becca Dingman, and Matt Huenerfauth. 2020. Reading Experiences and Interest in Reading-Assistance Tools Among Deaf and Hard-of-Hearing Computing Professionals. In *The 22nd International ACM SIGACCESS Conference on Computers and Accessibility*, pages 1–13, Virtual Event Greece. ACM.

S. E. Asch. 1946. Forming impressions of personality. *The Journal of Abnormal and Social Psychology*, 41(3):258–290.

Marion Bartl, Malvina Nissim, and Albert Gatt. 2020. Unmasking Contextual Stereotypes: Measuring and Mitigating BERT's Gender Bias. *arXiv:2010.14534 [cs]*.

Camiel J. Beukeboom and Christian Burgers. 2019. How Stereotypes Are Shared Through Language: A Review and Introduction of the Social Categories and Stereotypes Communication (SCSC) Framework. *Review of Communication Research*, 7(1):1–37.

Su Lin Blodgett. 2021. *Sociolinguistically Driven Approaches for Just Natural Language Processing*. Ph.D. thesis, University of Massachusetts Amherst.

Su Lin Blodgett, Solon Barocas, Hal Daumé III, and Hanna Wallach. 2020. Language (Technology) is Power: A Critical Survey of "Bias" in NLP. *arXiv:2005.14050 [cs]*.

Tolga Bolukbasi, Kai-Wei Chang, James Zou, Venkatesh Saligrama, and Adam Kalai. 2016. Man is to Computer Programmer as Woman is to Homemaker? Debiasing Word Embeddings. *arXiv:1607.06520 [cs, stat]*.

Aylin Caliskan, Joanna J. Bryson, and Arvind Narayanan. 2017. Semantics derived automatically from language corpora contain human-like biases. *Science*, 356(6334):183–186.

Yung-Sung Chuang, Chi-Liang Liu, Hung-yi Lee, and Lin-shan Lee. 2020. SpeechBERT: An Audio-and-Text Jointly Learned Language Model for End-to-End Spoken Question Answering. In *Interspeech 2020*, pages 4168–4172. ISCA.

Kimberlé Crenshaw. 1989. Demarginalizing the Intersection of Race and Sex: A Black Feminist Critique of Antidiscrimination Doctrine, Feminist Theory and Antiracist Politics. page 31.

Jacob Devlin, Ming-Wei Chang, Kenton Lee, and Kristina Toutanova. 2019. BERT: Pre-training of Deep Bidirectional Transformers for Language Understanding. In *Proceedings of the 2019 Conference of the North American Chapter of the Association for Computational Linguistics: Human Language Technologies, Volume 1 (Long and Short Papers)*, pages 4171–4186, Minneapolis, Minnesota. Association for Computational Linguistics.

Susan T. Fiske, Amy J. C. Cuddy, Peter Glick, and Jun Xu. 2002. A model of (often mixed) stereotype content: Competence and warmth respectively follow from perceived status and competition. *Journal of Personality and Social Psychology*, 82(6):878–902.

Susan T. Fiske, Amy J.C. Cuddy, and Peter Glick. 2007. Universal dimensions of social cognition: Warmth and competence. *Trends in Cognitive Sciences*, 11(2):77–83.

Kathleen C. Fraser, Isar Nejadgholi, and Svetlana Kiritchenko. 2021. Understanding and Countering Stereotypes: A Computational Approach to the Stereotype Content Model. In *Proceedings of the 59th Annual Meeting of the Association for Computational Linguistics and the 11th International Joint Conference on Natural Language Processing (Volume 1: Long Papers)*, pages 600–616, Online. Association for Computational Linguistics.

Eugenie Nicole Gertz. 2003. *Dysconscious Audism and Critical Deaf Studies: Deaf Crit's Analysis of Unconscious Internalization of Hegemony within the Deaf Community*. Ph.D. thesis.

Anthony G Greenwald, Debbie E McGhee, and Jordan L K Schwartz. 1998. Measuring Individual Differences in Implicit Cognition: The Implicit Association Test. page 17.

Saad Hassan, Matt Huenerfauth, and Cecilia Ovesdotter Alm. 2021. Unpacking the Interdependent Systems of Discrimination: Ableist Bias in NLP Systems through an Intersectional Lens. *arXiv:2110.00521 [cs]*.

Mark L Hatzenbuehler. 2016. Structural stigma: Research evidence and implications for psychological science. *American Psychologist*, 71(8):742.

Tom Humphries. 1977. *Communicating across cultures (deaf-hearing) and language learning*. Union Institute and University.

Ben Hutchinson, Vinodkumar Prabhakaran, Emily Denton, Kellie Webster, Yu Zhong, and Stephen Denuyl. 2020. Social Biases in NLP Models as Barriers for Persons with Disabilities. In *Proceedings of the 58th Annual Meeting of the Association for Computational Linguistics*, pages 5491–5501, Online. Association for Computational Linguistics.

Sushant Kafle, Abraham Glasser, Sedeeq Al-khazraji, Larwan Berke, Matthew Seita, and Matt Huenerfauth. 2019. Artificial intelligence fairness in the context of accessibility research on intelligent systems for people who are deaf or hard of hearing. *SIGACCESS*, (125).

Keita Kurita, Nidhi Vyas, Ayush Pareek, Alan W Black, and Yulia Tsvetkov. 2019. Measuring Bias in Contextualized Word Representations. In *Proceedings of the First Workshop on Gender Bias in Natural Language Processing*, pages 166–172, Florence, Italy. Association for Computational Linguistics.

Anne Lauscher, Ivan Vulić, Edoardo Maria Ponti, Anna Korhonen, and Goran Glavaš. 2020. Specializing Unsupervised Pretraining Models for Word-Level Semantic Similarity. In *Proceedings of the 28th International Conference on Computational Linguistics*, pages 1371–1383, Barcelona, Spain (Online). International Committee on Computational Linguistics.

Gandalf Nicolas, Xuechunzi Bai, and Susan T. Fiske. 2021. Comprehensive stereotype content dictionaries using a semi-automated method. *European Journal of Social Psychology*, 51(1):178–196.

Edlyn Vallejo Peña, Lissa D. Stapleton, and Lenore Malone Schaffer. 2016. Critical Perspectives on Disability Identity. *New Directions for Student Services*, 2016(154):85–96.

Alec Radford, Karthik Narasimhan, Tim Salimans, and Ilya Sutskever. 2018. Improving Language Understanding by Generative Pre-Training. page 12.

Alec Radford, Jeffrey Wu, Rewon Child, David Luan, Dario Amodei, and Ilya Sutskever. 2019. Language Models are Unsupervised Multitask Learners. page 24.

Timo Schick and Hinrich Schütze. 2020. Rare Words: A Major Problem for Contextualized Embeddings and How to Fix it by Attentive Mimicking. *Proceedings of the AAAI Conference on Artificial Intelligence*, 34(05):8766–8774.

Tom Shakespeare. 2016. The social model of disability. In Lennard J Davis, editor, *The Disability Studies Reader*, fifth edition, chapter 13, pages 190–199. Routledge.

Emily Sheng, Kai-Wei Chang, Premkumar Natarajan, and Nanyun Peng. 2020. Towards controllable biases in language generation. *arXiv preprint arXiv:2005.00268*.

Christen Szymanski. 2010. An open letter to training directors regarding accommodations for deaf interns. *AAPIC-E Newsletter*, 3(2):16–17.

Task Force Members and Contributors. 2012. Final report of the task force on health care careers for the deaf and hard-of-hearing community.

WHO. 2021. Disability and health. [Online; accessed 03-March-2022].

Wikipedia contributors. 2022. Wikipedia:wikiproject disability. [Online; accessed 03-March-2022].

Thomas Wolf, Lysandre Debut, Victor Sanh, Julien Chaumond, Clement Delangue, Anthony Moi, Pierric Cistac, Tim Rault, Rémi Louf, Morgan Funtowicz, Joe Davison, Sam Shleifer, Patrick von Platen, Clara Ma, Yacine Jernite, Julien Plu, Canwen Xu, Teven Le Scao, Sylvain Gugger, Mariama Drame, Quentin Lhoest, and Alexander M. Rush. 2020. HuggingFace's Transformers: State-of-the-art Natural Language Processing. *arXiv:1910.03771 [cs]*.

CueBot: Cue-Controlled Response Generation for Assistive Interaction Usages

Shachi H Kumar, Hsuan Su*, Ramesh Manuvinakurike*,
Maximilian C Pinaroc, Sai Prasad, Saurav Sahay and Lama Nachman
Intel Labs, Santa Clara, CA, USA
{shachi.h.kumar, hsuan.su, ramesh.manuvinakurike,
maximilian.c.pinaroc, sai.prasad, saurav.sahay, lama.nachman }@intel.com

Abstract

Conversational assistants are ubiquitous among the general population, however, these systems have not had an impact on people with disabilities, or speech and language disorders, for whom basic day-to-day communication and social interaction is a huge struggle. Language model technology can play a huge role in empowering these users and help them interact with others with less effort via interaction support. To enable this population, we build a system that can represent them in a social conversation and generate responses that can be controlled by the users using cues/keywords. For an ongoing conversation, this system can suggest responses that a user can choose. We also build models that can speed up this communication by suggesting relevant cues in the dialog response context. We introduce a keyword-loss to lexically constrain the model response output. We present automatic and human evaluation of our cue/keyword predictor and the controllable dialog system to show that our models perform significantly better than models without control. Our evaluation and user study shows that keyword-control on end-to-end response generation models is powerful and can enable and empower users with degenerative disorders to carry out their day-to-day communication.

1 Introduction

Conversational agents such as Google Home and Alexa have become almost an integral part of homes and used by people of all ages to carry out tasks such as setting reminders, playing music and accessing information. There are also agents that can simply engage in chit-chat conversations, however, these open domain conversational agents have mostly been research explorations (Ram et al., 2018). Large-scale pre-training has attained significant performance gains across many tasks within Language Modeling (Devlin et al., 2019; Radford and Narasimhan, 2018), including intent prediction (Castellucci et al., 2019; Chen et al., 2019b) and dialogue state tracking (Heck et al., 2020). These pretrained language models have demonstrated surprising generality in open domain dialog tasks, with models like DialoGPT (Zhang et al., 2020b), Meena (Adiwardana et al., 2020) and BlenderBot (Roller et al., 2020) achieving performance competitive with humans in certain settings. With the availability of these models, novel products and applications are emerging (Bommasani et al., 2021) such as Communication Systems (eg. email response completion (Chen et al., 2019a)), Creativity Tools (story writing assistance (Roemmele and Gordon, 2018; Roemmele, 2021)), Human-AI collaboration for Software Engineering (Chen et al., 2021), biosciences (protein structure prediction (Rives et al., 2020) and several others.

One such accessibility application we are exploring is aimed towards leveraging language modeling technology to support minority group of people with certain disabilities [1] to communicate with others effectively. For example, Amyotrophic Lateral Sclerosis (ALS) is a progressive, degenerative, neurological disorder, where people lose their muscle movement, voice and the ability to carry out a normal day-to-day conversation. It takes huge effort and time for these patients to use existing systems [2] to communicate sentences character by character using various data input mechanisms available to them (gaze, fingers, muscle movements). Henceforth, we will use the term 'user' for such patients with disabilities, for whom our system is intended to support.

Our goal is to empower these users to communicate faster by having an intelligent agent be their voice and reduce the silence gap in the conversation resulting from users slower keystroke inputs.

*These authors contributed equally to this work

[1] According to WHO, there are more than 1 Billion people with disabilities

[2] https://01.org/ACAT

Ninth Workshop on Speech and Language Processing for Assistive Technologies (SLPAT-2022), pages 66 - 79
May 27, 2022 ©2022 Association for Computational Linguistics

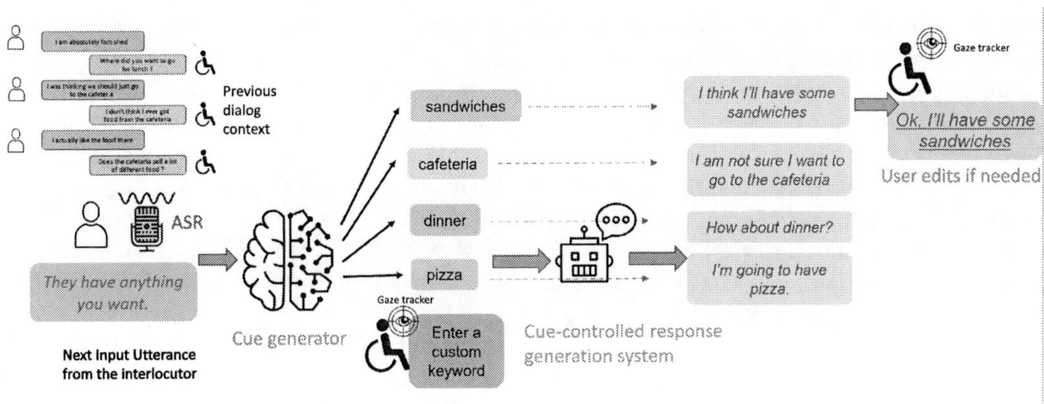

Figure 1: A dialog system for an assistive use-case can listen to a conversation and provide diverse cues to the user. These cues, provide human control to the dialog system that can generate relevant responses that could be edited.

The system needs to listen to an ongoing conversation (using automatic speech recognition(ASR)) and should use be able to use very limited user input and suggest responses that can be interactively chosen and edited for near real time social interactions. Such a system needs to be context-aware (contexts such as ongoing conversations, user's emotions, environment), personalized (language usage and style of the user and also be aware of users' interests/likes and dislikes) and most importantly, controllable. In this work, we focus on the controllability aspect and design the control mechanism via keywords in the system. We present the following contributions: i) **Minority Group Application:** We bring forth a novel usage for response generation systems, i.e., to represent users with disabilities and help them in their day-to-day communication needs. ii) **Minimal user intervention:** We present a human-controllable response generation using keywords/cues. We also build keyword/cue predictor models that further speed up communication time and evaluate these. iii) **Keyword Loss:** We introduce a keyword loss to our training objective that further helps in incorporating soft lexical constraints in the form of keywords/similar words in the generated responses, validated through automatic and human evaluation. We also present a user-study to understand the usefullness and the effectivness of our overall system.

Figure 1 shows the interaction flow of our system. An ASR system converts an ongoing conversation (between an interlocutor and a user with disabilities) to text, which is input to the cue/keyword generator that generates possible, relevant cues that the user might want to respond with. The user can choose one of these keywords or also enter his/her own keyword to control the system. This keyword is an input to the response generator model that can generate relevant responses based on the keyword. The user can then either use one of the suggested responses or edit a response with just a few keystrokes, thus drastically reducing communication time.

2 Related Work

Assistive Technologies: Various AI technologies have proven to be helpful for people with limited mobility, hearing capabilities and speech impairments. (Brady et al., 2013; Guo et al., 2020; MacLeod et al., 2017; Elakkiya, 2020; Mišeikis et al., 2020; Ozawa et al., 2020; Ramli et al., 2020; Shor et al., 2019). People with ALS need Augmentative and Alternative Communication (AAC) strategies to address and support daily communication, such as speech generation (Beukelman et al., 2011), eye-tracking tools (Gibbons and Beneteau, 2010) and Brain Computer Interaction (BCI) interfaces (Wolpaw et al., 2018). (Linse et al., 2018). Current systems use interfaces with inputs via eyegaze, touch or BCI (Orhan et al., 2011) with some predictive text capability and some systems using simpler n-gram based language models (Verbally, 2021; TherapyBox, 2021) and do not exploit the potential of using response generation technology using deep learning based language models. There has also been some work on collecting AAC communication data for language modeling (Vertanen, 2013), (Vertanen and Kristensson, 2011). While this data could be used to support single-turn retrieval-based dialog systems, these do not support multi-turn dialog response generation. To the best of our knowledge, there aren't many research explorations for conversational technology based applications that exploit the latest language modeling techniques for people with ALS.

Controllable Generation: Controllability in text generation and dialog systems has emerged as an active research area. (Keskar et al., 2019) pre-train a conditional transformer model with different types of control codes. (Xu et al., 2020b) and (Xu et al., 2020a) presents a keyword controlled story and dialog generation respectively. While (Ghazvininejad et al., 2017; See et al., 2019) use post-processing techniques to control generated text, (Dathathri et al., 2020) present a plug-and-play architecture, where the base language model is untouched and small attribute models induce control, further extended in (Madotto et al., 2020). (Smith et al., 2020) and (Gupta et al., 2020) control generation using style and semantic exemplars. However, these controllable attributes are too broad and not suitable for our use-case. These techniques also require a lot of computational resources which is not feasible in real-time assistive applications.

Similarity-based Loss Function: For improving the generated response, some recent work has focused on addressing the loss functions during model training. (Kovaleva et al., 2018) use similarity-based losses to enhance the diversity and meaning in the generated sentence. (Sha, 2020) aims to lexically constrain the language generation at word level. In our work, we aim to compute the loss across the entire sentence to guide keyword generation.

3 Keyword and Response Modeling

3.1 Controllability using cues/keywords

In order to make response generation controllable with minimum user-intervention, we incorporate cues/keywords as input control to generate relevant responses to a given dialog context. We enable keyword-control by 1) providing automatically generated keywords as auxillary input to the model and 2) by introducing a novel keyword-based loss that encourages the model to generate sentences containing the keyword or words semantically similar to the keyword. In the working system, the keyword is either entered by the user or selected by the user from a set of provided options. To generate data to train such a model, given a conversation context and a response output, we automatically extract keywords from the responses using keyBERT (Grootendorst, 2020) and use the HuggingFace TransferTransfo model (Wolf et al., 2019) as our base architecture. We use the top 1-gram keyword for each dialog response, and use both single keywords and multiple keywords as inputs.

3.1.1 Keywords as context

For a given conversation context, we incorporate keywords into the TransferTransfo model by adding new keyword-specific-tokens, in addition to dialog-state/speaker tokens that represent speaker turns in the dialog. We further extend the dialog-state embeddings to add 'keyword-state-embeddings' with special keyword separator token to indicate the positions of the keyword tokens.

3.1.2 Keyword-based loss functions

We propose keyword-based loss functions that encourage the occurence of the input keyword(s) in the generated sentence. We introduce variations to this loss function to enable the generation of semantically similar word to the input keyword as well as incorporate multiple-keyword inputs as control to the model. With addition of this loss, the overall loss of the model is a combination of : language model loss L_m, next sentence prediction loss L_n (both part of the TransferTransfo architecture) and keyword loss L_k,

$$\text{Overall Loss, } L = \alpha L_m + \beta L_n + \gamma L_k \tag{1}$$

where α, β and the γ are the hyper-parameters.

Keyword Loss: In order to encourage the generation of the cue/keyword in a sentence, we maximize the similarity between the keyword, kw, and one of the generated words (at some output position). From the probability distribution (generated logits), we compute the negative log of the probability of the keyword (p_i) at every timestep i=1 to T. We then take the minimum of these scores across the generated sentence as the loss w.r.t keyword K,

$$L_k = \min_{i=1}^{T}(-\log p_i(kw)), \tag{2}$$

Keyword Loss with similar words: We incorporate embedding-based similarity scores into the keyword loss computation as shown in equation 3 in order to encourage generation of not just the keywords, but also semantically similar words in the sentence. Let $pool = kw \cup sim\_words(kw)$.

The Keyword loss L_k,

$$L_k = sim(k, kw) \min_{i=1}^{T}(-\log p_i(k)), \quad \text{where } k = \arg\min_{x \in pool}(\min_{i=1}^{T}(-\log p_i(x))) \tag{3}$$

Keyword Loss with multiple inputs : Consider $k_1, k_2 ... k_N$ as the N multiple control inputs, where it is desirable that the generated output contains all of the keywords (or similar words). To enable this, we minimize the negative log probability for each keyword, k_j, across the entire sentence and add these scores as the total loss.

$$L_k = \sum_{j=1}^{N} \min_{i=1}^{T}(-\log p_i(k_j)) \tag{4}$$

3.2 Keyword Generation

While keyword-controlled responses reduce the interaction time significantly, we try to further improve the experience and minimize the latency by automatically suggesting keywords to the user. We build two types of models:

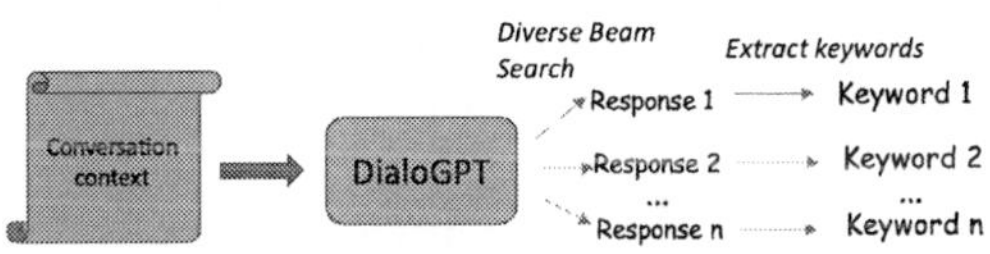

Figure 2: Extractive Keyword Predictor

1) Extractive keyword predictor: Figure 2 shows the extractive keyword predictor. Given a conversation context, we use DialoGPT(Zhang et al., 2020c) with diverse beam search(Vijayakumar et al., 2018) to generate multiple responses (we use 10 beams, 2 groups and diversity_penalty of 5.5). We then use keyBERT(Grootendorst, 2020) to extract keywords from the beam outputs and present these as keyword suggestions.

2) Generative keyword predictor: To train a generative keyword predictor, we finetune GPT2 using a conversation context as input and keywords from the ground truth response as output. Figure 3 shows this process. The model generates multiple keywords for a given context using diverse beam search and presents these as suggestions. Keywords are extracted from the DailyDialog dataset (Li et al., 2017) to create the data to train the keyword predictor.

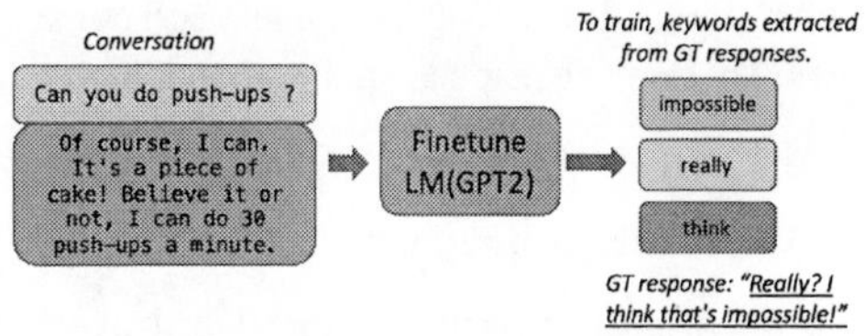

Figure 3: Generative Keyword Predictor

4 Experimental Setup

We initialize the TransferTransfo architecture weights of DialoGPT 'medium' model with 345M parameters. Language modeling and multiclass-classification coefficients, α and β are set to 1 as in the original model. We use a batch_size of 64 for training, nucleus sampling for generation with top_p set to 0.9 to fine-tune the model for 3 epochs. We run an ablation study to determine the effect of different ways of incorporating keywords using 5 main classes of models: i) No-keyword model (no_kw): Trained without any keyword information ii) Keyword-context ($kw\_context$): Trained with keyword as auxillary input + dialog context iii) Keyword-loss (kw_loss): Incorporates keyword loss + keyword as auxillary information. iv) Keyword sim-loss (kw_sim_loss): Incorporate similar words (embedding-based techniques such as Glove (Pennington et al., 2014) ($kw\_sim\_loss\_glove$) and wordnet-based ($kw\_sim\_loss\_wordnet$) similarity) for loss computation . We experiment with 2 variations, one using the similarity score, and the other using 1. v) Multiple-keyword-loss ($multi\_kw\_loss$): Incorporate multiple keywords into the input as well as into the loss computation.

4.1 Datasets

Although there are a few AAC datasets, (Vertanen and Kristensson, 2011), (Vertanen, 2013), they lack multi-turn dialogs, which is central to our task as well as our use-case. Hence we use the Dailydialog dataset (Li et al., 2017), which consists of 13,118 daily conversations involving various topics such as tourism, culture, education, etc., with the goal of exchanging ideas and information and enhancing social bonding. The dataset includes conversations around health, ordinary life and emotions among others, which allows it to serve as a staring point for building systems to support social communication for AAC applications. We use the test set, consisting of 6740 context-response pairs, to evaluate our models.

4.2 Automatic Evaluation

Given the well-discussed fact that word-overlap based metrics do not agree well with human judgment, we utilize learning based and embedding-based metrics to evaluate the generated response with the reference ground truth.

4.2.1 Metrics for Evaluating Keyword Predictor Models

The keyword predictor model should be able to generate diverse keywords to present varied options for users to choose from. We evalute the extractive and generative keyword predictors using averaged cosine similarity between generated keywords as a measure of diversity-lower the similarity, higher the diversity. We hypothesize that meaningful keywords will result in generation of meaningful and context-relevant responses. Hence, we use these keywords to generate responses, and score the responses based on 'human-like' and coherence scores using DialogRPT (Gao et al., 2020), a model trained to predict human feedback dialogue responses.

4.2.2 Metrics for Evaluating Controllable Response Generation Model

Keyword Insertion Accuracy(KIA): The main goal of this work is to provide fine-grained control to the user and have the model induce a keyword or a similar word in the response. To objectively evaluate this, we define keyword-insertion accuracy, where we identify if the input word or a word that is similar, is a part of the generated sentence or not. We compute the accuracy of exact keyword insertion and we also compute accuracies of insertion of words containing similar meaning into the generated response. We use embedding-based cosine similarity metrics and heuristically use a threshold 0.7 to compute the accuracies.

Similarity-Based & Response Quality Metrics Since we intend to generate keyword-based responses, computing measures of similarity between the generated response and ground truth using metrics such as BLEURT, BERTScore (Zhang et al., 2020a) (Sellam et al., 2020), Sentence-BERT (Reimers and Gurevych, 2019) gives a good assessment for the model performance.

We evaluate turn level response quality aspects such as fluency and context coherence using language model based evaluation (GPT-2) and diversity using n-gram based evaluation (Pang et al., 2020) [3]. We also measure the perpelexity (PPL) by employing pretrained GPT-2 "medium".

4.3 Human Evaluation

We perform human evaluation via Amazon Mechanical Turk(AMT) to evaluate the keyword predictor models and controllable response generation models in 3 separate crowd-tasks.

Task1: Collecting response for automatic and human-entered keywords We present a conversation context and keywords (from the extractive and generative keyword prediction models) to the turkers and ask them to come up with possible responses relevant to these keywords. To represent human-control in our analysis, the turkers are also asked to enter keywords of their choice, along with the corresponding responses. We use these in Task 2 to present to the turkers as human responses.

Task2: Overall system interaction and metrics: In the interaction flow, the user reads the conversation context, picks a keyword (From task 1) that he/she wants to respond with - which brings up a human response (from Task1) and a model response (kw_loss model). The user can use a response as is or edit or type a new response altogether. We analyse if the users tend to choose a model or a human response and also compute the word error rates (WER) for the corresponding edits.

Task3: Human Evaluation of controllable response generation models: We randomly pick 100 dialog contexts and present the context along with the keyword and pairs of responses from the models and ask 3 annotators to rate the responses based on the following criteria: 1) Fluency: how natural and fluent the responses are, 2) Generic: are the responses too generic given the dialog context?, 3) Context relevance: how relevant and coherent is a response to a given dialog context, 4) Keyword relevance: relevance of a response to the keyword.

We present pairs of responses from models A and B and provide 4 options for each of the above criteria: A better than B, B better than A, Both and, Neither. We evaluate the pairs, $no\_keyword$ vs $kw\_context$, $no\_keyword$ vs kw_loss and

[3]https://github.com/alexzhou907/dialogue_evaluation

Kw Predictor	Coherence	Human-like	Diversity↓
Generative	**0.903**	**0.641**	**0.227**
Extractive	0.891	0.595	0.265

Table 1: Evaluation of keyword predictor models.

kw_context vs *kw_loss*. We compute the scores using a majority vote across 3 annotators.

5 Results and Discussion

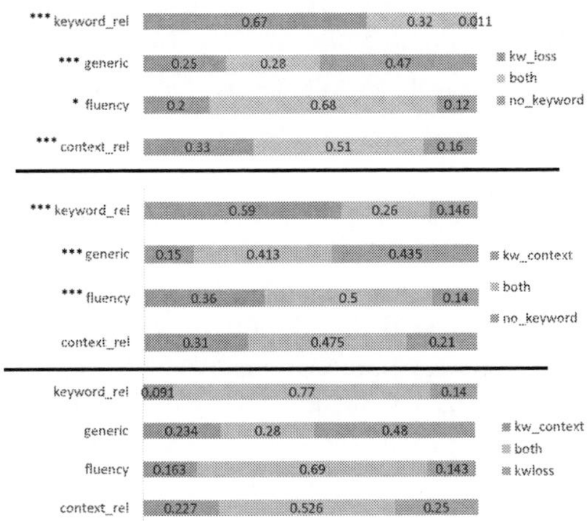

Figure 4: Results from human evaluation. (One-Sample Wilcoxon Signed Rank Test (mu=0) for the statistical tests.*** p<0.001, ** p<0.01, * p<0.05.)

5.1 Automatic Evaluation Results

Keyword Predictor Models: Table 1 shows that the generative keyword predictor tends to generate more diverse keywords (lower score of cosine similarity indicates higher diversity), which is very important in our use-case. The generated responses are also more coherent and human-like.

Cue/Keyword controlled models: We experiment the keyword-loss models with various values of γ ranging between 0 and 1 and see the best performance when γ=0.005. Henceforth, we use keyword-loss models with γ=0.005 for all our experiments.From Table 2, the KIA for the *no_kw* model is very low, given the one to many nature of open domain dialog. By guiding the model with keywords, the KIA goes up to 67.2% and this is improved to 69.4% in *kw_loss* model. All of the cue/keyword based models outperform the *no_kw* model in all of the similarity-based and response quality metrics, except perplexity where the *no_kw* model is the best. Adding keyword-loss greatly improves the context coherence and fluency as compared to adding keyword as context information alone. The context coherence is the highest when we use similarity-based keyword loss, which encourages generating sentences with words having similar meaning as the input word. The *kw_simloss_glove* − 1 and *kw_simloss_wordnet* − 1 models also show better performance as compared to the *kw_context* model. Table 2 also shows the results on using multiple keywords input. We observe that KIA improves with the *kw_loss* models, especially the glove-similarity based model.

5.2 Human Evaluation Results

We collect about 1000 responses for the keywords suggested by the two keyword predictors and also collect 1000 additional human keywords and corresponding responses from Task 1.

On analysing the response choice (human vs model generated) of the turkers in Task 2, we find that from 121 interactions, 34.7% of the interactions used model response, and 29.7% used human response. We also observe that 60 interactions result in edits of the response. Out of this, the WER for edits for a human response is 0.45 while WER for edits is lower when a model response is chosen, at 0.39. This further indicates that the model response is closer to what the user wants to convey.

Figure 4 shows the human ratings for response quality metrics for different models. We observe that the *kw_loss* and *kw_context* models outperform the model without control, on all metrics. The keyword-based models generate more fluent and relevant responses. We also observe that humans rate *kw_context* and *kw_loss* models as very comparable, with *kw_loss* models being more keyword and context relevant as also established by the automatic evaluations.

5.3 User Study

We perform a preliminary study with 7 users[4] by mimicking the disability scenario where the user can only interact with the system using eye-gaze as input. The user interface is controlled using a commercial eye-gaze tracker that works along with an open source mouse-control software, OptiKey[5], an on-screen keyboard designed for users

[4] pandemic, limited hardware availability among other socio-technical issues impedes the pace of the study

[5] https://github.com/OptiKey/OptiKey

	KIA	Similarity	BLEURT	BERT Score	Context	Diversity	Fluency	PPL↓
Single Keyword								
no_kw	0.083	0.271	-1.035	0.868/0.836/0.851	0.541	1.592	**0.407**	**39.098**
kw_context	0.672	0.539	-0.607	0.844/0.853/0.868	0.568	**1.789**	0.403	41.752
kw_loss	**0.694**	**0.542**	-0.609	**0.885/0.852/0.868**	0.579	1.726	**0.407**	43.115
kw_sim_loss_glove-1	0.684	0.541	**-0.606**	0.884/0.852/0.868	**0.585**	1.729	0.405	42.544
kw_sim_loss_wordnet-1	0.686	0.540	-0.615	0.884/0.852/0.868	0.581	1.726	0.403	42.606
kw_sim_loss_glove	0.680	0.543	-0.610	0.885/0.852/0.868	0.570	1.741	0.403	42.362
kw_sim_loss_wordnet	0.672	0.541	-0.606	0.884/0.852/0.867	0.576	1.733	0.403	42.301
Multiple Keywords								
no_kw	0.041	0.271	-1.035	0.868/0.836/0.851	0.541	1.592	0.407	**39.098**
kw_context	0.293	0.607	**-0.499**	**0.895/0.857/0.875**	0.489	**1.396**	0.399	75.300
kw_loss	0.300	0.604	-0.524	0.894/0.856/0.874	**0.492**	1.354	0.412	83.971
kw_sim_loss_glove-1	**0.302**	**0.610**	-0.535	**0.895/0.857/0.875**	0.487	1.366	0.416	84.367

Table 2: Performance of the various controllable models for single and multi-keyword inputs ($\gamma = 0.005$). Label "-1" indicates that we set $sim(k, kw) = 1$ in equation 3.

with Motor neurone disease(MND). The user interacts with a wizard-based interlocutor in a multi-turn dialog to complete open ended conversation goals. Users can pick two goals/tasks to complete (which the wizard is unaware of) out of sample tasks. After completion of the two tasks, the users are required to answer a survey with likert-scale questions where they rate the overall experience in the task. From the survey, we find that the users "felt that the provided tasks were meaningful and the keywords were very useful in carrying out the communication". The users also reported that they used the generated responses as it was 'very close to what they wanted to say' (one-tail t-test, mu= 0, mean=0.5, $p < 0.05$). Users appreciated that the study made them empathize with users for whom basic communication is a struggle. Some feedback from users: "*Typing a whole sentence character by character can be painful*", "*The keyword suggestion and response generation feature were quite useful as it cuts down significant efforts from user's side*", "*The responses were pretty good. keywords were sometimes not useful and not what I wanted to convey. I hoped that Spiderman would show up as a movie suggestion just when I entered spider(as it was hard to type) and it worked! that was good to see!*"

6 Conclusion

We present a novel usage for open domain conversational models - representing differently abled users and enabling them to communicate. In such a use-case, minimizing the need for user intervention is critical, hence the focus of this work has been to develop controllable response generation models that enable fine-grained human control in the form of keyword inputs from the user. We also introduce keyword-based loss functions that encourages the model to generate the keyword or similar words in the response. To further improve efficiency and time in interaction, we develop keyword predictors and evaluate them. We show with both automatic and human evaluation that our models outperform the baseline model with no control, at the same time maintaining the response quality. We are working with patients to collect feedback and plan to deploy our system as part of an open source tool to impact the quality of life of the patients and help the caregivers. Future research direction also involves improving the keyword predictors, and personalization of these controllable models (both speech and linguistic).

7 Ethics

CueBot aims to support users with neurological disorders in day-to-day communication while also enabling them to control the response generation. The system has been extensively evaluated using automatic metrics as well as human evaluation via AMT, where the AMT workers were fairly compensated (average >$15 per hour). One of the AMT tasks included rating of responses generated from our models and from humans. We tried to mitigate any bias that could arise in the choices made by turkers by constantly shuffling the responses that we presented. We did not collect any additional personal details (other than those collect by AMT by default) or identities from AMT workers' for any of our tasks, hence preserving their privacy. As next steps, we plan to use the feedback from our user study to improve the system, and integrate into ACAT to enable user studies with ALS patients and further gain their feedback to improve the AI modules. In the current system we use google ASR for the interlocuters speech, which raises some privacy concerns. To mitigate this, we plan to use a local ASR system rather than a cloud ASR so that the data is processed locally. To enable this, we need to evaluate the performance of local ASR systems against the cloud-based google ASR. Both the keyword suggestion and response generation modules use pre-trained language models such as GPT2 and DialoGPT finetuned on DailyDialog dataset conversations. Given this, the responses generated could possibly contain improper content or bias due to the large dataset these models are pre-trained on. This raises some important ethical questions that we intend to tackle as part of future work. In this current work we have not explored bias mitigation, which will also be a part of future work.

References

D. Adiwardana, Minh-Thang Luong, D. So, J. Hall, Noah Fiedel, R. Thoppilan, Z. Yang, Apoorv Kulshreshtha, Gaurav Nemade, Yifeng Lu, and Quoc V. Le. 2020. Towards a human-like open-domain chatbot. *ArXiv*, abs/2001.09977.

David Beukelman, Susan Fager, and Amy Nordness. 2011. Communication support for people with als. *Neurology research international*, 2011:714693.

Rishi Bommasani, Drew A. Hudson, Ehsan Adeli, Russ Altman, et al. 2021. On the opportunities and risks of foundation models.

Erin Brady, Meredith Ringel Morris, Yu Zhong, Samuel White, and Jeffrey P. Bigham. 2013. Visual challenges in the everyday lives of blind people. In *Proceedings of the SIGCHI Conference on Human Factors in Computing Systems*, CHI '13, page 2117–2126, New York, NY, USA. Association for Computing Machinery.

Giuseppe Castellucci, Valentina Bellomaria, A. Favalli, and R. Romagnoli. 2019. Multi-lingual intent detection and slot filling in a joint bert-based model. *ArXiv*, abs/1907.02884.

Mark Chen, Jerry Tworek, Heewoo Jun, Qiming Yuan, Henrique Ponde de Oliveira Pinto, Jared Kaplan, Harri Edwards, Yuri Burda, Nicholas Joseph, Greg Brockman, Alex Ray, Raul Puri, Gretchen Krueger, Michael Petrov, Heidy Khlaaf, Girish Sastry, Pamela Mishkin, Brooke Chan, Scott Gray, Nick Ryder, Mikhail Pavlov, Alethea Power, Lukasz Kaiser, Mohammad Bavarian, Clemens Winter, Philippe Tillet, Felipe Petroski Such, Dave Cummings, Matthias Plappert, Fotios Chantzis, Elizabeth Barnes, Ariel Herbert-Voss, William Hebgen Guss, Alex Nichol, Alex Paino, Nikolas Tezak, Jie Tang, Igor Babuschkin, Suchir Balaji, Shantanu Jain, William Saunders, Christopher Hesse, Andrew N. Carr, Jan Leike, Josh Achiam, Vedant Misra, Evan Morikawa, Alec Radford, Matthew Knight, Miles Brundage, Mira Murati, Katie Mayer, Peter Welinder, Bob McGrew, Dario Amodei, Sam McCandlish, Ilya Sutskever, and Wojciech Zaremba. 2021. Evaluating large language models trained on code.

Mia Xu Chen, Benjamin N. Lee, Gagan Bansal, Yuan Cao, Shuyuan Zhang, Justin Lu, Jackie Tsay, Yinan Wang, Andrew M. Dai, Zhifeng Chen, Timothy Sohn, and Yonghui Wu. 2019a. Gmail smart compose: Real-time assisted writing. In *Proceedings of the 25th ACM SIGKDD International Conference on Knowledge Discovery and Data Mining*, KDD '19, page 2287–2295, New York, NY, USA. Association for Computing Machinery.

Qian Chen, Zhu Zhuo, and W. Wang. 2019b. Bert for joint intent classification and slot filling. *ArXiv*, abs/1902.10909.

Sumanth Dathathri, Andrea Madotto, Janice Lan, Jane Hung, Eric Frank, Piero Molino, Jason Yosinski, and Rosanne Liu. 2020. Plug and play language models: A simple approach to controlled text generation. In *8th International Conference on Learning Representations, ICLR 2020, Addis Ababa, Ethiopia, April 26-30, 2020*. OpenReview.net.

Jacob Devlin, Ming-Wei Chang, Kenton Lee, and Kristina Toutanova. 2019. BERT: Pre-training of deep bidirectional transformers for language understanding. In *Proceedings of the 2019 Conference of the North American Chapter of the Association for Computational Linguistics: Human Language Technologies, Volume 1 (Long and Short Papers)*, pages 4171–4186, Minneapolis, Minnesota. Association for Computational Linguistics.

R. Elakkiya. 2020. Machine learning based sign language recognition: a review and its research frontier. *Journal of Ambient Intelligence and Humanized Computing*.

Xiang Gao, Yizhe Zhang, Michel Galley, Chris Brockett, and Bill Dolan. 2020. Dialogue response ranking-training with large-scale human feedback data. In *EMNLP*.

Marjan Ghazvininejad, Xing Shi, Jay Priyadarshi, and Kevin Knight. 2017. Hafez: an interactive poetry generation system. In *Proceedings of ACL 2017, System Demonstrations*, pages 43–48, Vancouver, Canada. Association for Computational Linguistics.

Chris Gibbons and Erin Beneteau. 2010. Functional performance using eye control and single switch scanning by people with als. *Perspectives on Augmentative and Alternative Communication*, 19(3):64–69.

Maarten Grootendorst. 2020. Keybert: Minimal keyword extraction with bert.

Anhong Guo, Ece Kamar, Jennifer Wortman Vaughan, Hanna Wallach, and Meredith Ringel Morris. 2020. Toward fairness in ai for people with disabilities sbg@a research roadmap. *SIGACCESS Access. Comput.*, (125).

Prakhar Gupta, Jeffrey P. Bigham, Yulia Tsvetkov, and Amy Pavel. 2020. Controlling dialogue generation with semantic exemplars. *CoRR*, abs/2008.09075.

Michael Heck, Carel van Niekerk, Nurul Lubis, Christian Geishauser, Hsien-Chin Lin, Marco Moresi, and Milica Gasic. 2020. TripPy: A triple copy strategy for value independent neural dialog state tracking. In *Proceedings of the 21th Annual Meeting of the Special Interest Group on Discourse and Dialogue*, pages 35–44, 1st virtual meeting. Association for Computational Linguistics.

Nitish Shirish Keskar, Bryan McCann, Lav R. Varshney, Caiming Xiong, and Richard Socher. 2019. CTRL: A conditional transformer language model for controllable generation. *CoRR*, abs/1909.05858.

Olga Kovaleva, Anna Rumshisky, and Alexey Romanov. 2018. Similarity-based reconstruction loss for meaning representation. In *Proceedings of the 2018 Conference on Empirical Methods in Natural Language Processing*, pages 4875–4880, Brussels, Belgium. Association for Computational Linguistics.

Yanran Li, Hui Su, Xiaoyu Shen, Wenjie Li, Ziqiang Cao, and Shuzi Niu. 2017. Dailydialog: A manually labelled multi-turn dialogue dataset. In *Proceedings of the Eighth International Joint Conference on Natural Language Processing, IJCNLP 2017, Taipei, Taiwan, November 27 - December 1, 2017 - Volume 1: Long Papers*, pages 986–995. Asian Federation of Natural Language Processing.

Katharina Linse, Elisa Aust, Markus Joos, and Andreas Hermann. 2018. Communication matters—pitfalls and promise of hightech communication devices in palliative care of severely physically disabled patients with amyotrophic lateral sclerosis. *Frontiers in Neurology*, 9:603.

Haley MacLeod, Cynthia L. Bennett, Meredith Ringel Morris, and Edward Cutrell. 2017. Understanding blind people's experiences with computer-generated captions of social media images. In *Proceedings of the 2017 CHI Conference on Human Factors in Computing Systems*, CHI '17, page 5988–5999, New York, NY, USA. Association for Computing Machinery.

Andrea Madotto, Etsuko Ishii, Zhaojiang Lin, Sumanth Dathathri, and Pascale Fung. 2020. Plug-and-play conversational models. In *Proceedings of the 2020 Conference on Empirical Methods in Natural Language Processing: Findings, EMNLP 2020, Online Event, 16-20 November 2020*, pages 2422–2433. Association for Computational Linguistics.

J. Mišeikis, P. Caroni, P. Duchamp, A. Gasser, R. Marko, N. Mišeikienė, F. Zwilling, C. de Castelbajac, L. Eicher, M. Früh, and H. Früh. 2020. Lio-a personal robot assistant for human-robot interaction and care applications. *IEEE Robotics and Automation Letters*, 5(4):5339–5346.

Umut Orhan, Deniz Erdogmus, Brian Roark, Shalini Purwar, Kenneth E. Hild II, Barry Oken, Hooman Nezamfar, and Melanie Fried-Oken. 2011. Fusion with language models improves spelling accuracy for erp-based brain computer interface spellers. In *33rd Annual International Conference of the IEEE Engineering in Medicine and Biology Society, EMBC 2011, Boston, MA, USA, August 30 - Sept. 3, 2011*, pages 5774–5777. IEEE.

Kuniaki Ozawa, Masayoshi Naito, Naoki Tanaka, and Shiryu Wada. 2020. A word communication system with caregiver assist for amyotrophic lateral sclerosis patients in completely and almost completely locked-in state.

Bo Pang, Erik Nijkamp, Wenjuan Han, Linqi Zhou, Yixian Liu, and Kewei Tu. 2020. Towards holistic and automatic evaluation of open-domain dialogue generation. In *Proceedings of the 58th Annual Meeting of the Association for Computational Linguistics, ACL 2020, Online, July 5-10, 2020*, pages 3619–3629. Association for Computational Linguistics.

Jeffrey Pennington, Richard Socher, and Christopher D. Manning. 2014. Glove: Global vectors for word representation. In *Empirical Methods in Natural Language Processing (EMNLP)*, pages 1532–1543.

A. Radford and Karthik Narasimhan. 2018. Improving language understanding by generative pre-training.

Ashwin Ram, Rohit Prasad, Chandra Khatri, Anu Venkatesh, Raefer Gabriel, Qing Liu, Jeff Nunn, Behnam Hedayatnia, Ming Cheng, Ashish Nagar, Eric King, Kate Bland, Amanda Wartick, Yi Pan, Han Song, Sk Jayadevan, Gene Hwang, and Art Pettigrue. 2018. Conversational ai: The science behind the alexa prize.

Albara Ah Ramli, Rex Liu, Rahul Krishnamoorthy, I. B. Vishal, Xiaoxiao Wang, Ilias Tagkopoulos, and Xin Liu. 2020. Bwcnn: Blink to word, a real-time convolutional neural network approach. *Internet of Things - ICIOT 2020*, page 133–140.

Nils Reimers and Iryna Gurevych. 2019. Sentence-bert: Sentence embeddings using siamese bert-networks. In *Proceedings of the 2019 Conference on Empirical Methods in Natural Language Processing and the 9th International Joint Conference on Natural Language Processing, EMNLP-IJCNLP 2019, Hong Kong, China, November 3-7, 2019*, pages 3980–3990. Association for Computational Linguistics.

Alexander Rives, Joshua Meier, Tom Sercu, Siddharth Goyal, Zeming Lin, Jason Liu, Demi Guo, Myle Ott, C. Lawrence Zitnick, Jerry Ma, and Rob Fergus.

2020. Biological structure and function emerge from scaling unsupervised learning to 250 million protein sequences. *bioRxiv*.

Melissa Roemmele. 2021. Inspiration through observation: Demonstrating the influence of automatically generated text on creative writing. *arXiv preprint arXiv:2107.04007*.

Melissa Roemmele and Andrew S Gordon. 2018. Automated assistance for creative writing with an rnn language model. In *Proceedings of the 23rd International Conference on Intelligent User Interfaces Companion*, pages 1–2.

Stephen Roller, Emily Dinan, Naman Goyal, Da Ju, Mary Williamson, Yinhan Liu, Jing Xu, Myle Ott, Kurt Shuster, Eric Smith, Y-Lan Boureau, and Jason Weston. 2020. Recipes for building an open-domain chatbot.

Abigail See, Stephen Roller, Douwe Kiela, and Jason Weston. 2019. What makes a good conversation? how controllable attributes affect human judgments. In *Proceedings of the 2019 Conference of the North American Chapter of the Association for Computational Linguistics: Human Language Technologies, Volume 1 (Long and Short Papers)*, pages 1702–1723, Minneapolis, Minnesota. Association for Computational Linguistics.

Thibault Sellam, Dipanjan Das, and Ankur P. Parikh. 2020. BLEURT: learning robust metrics for text generation. In *Proceedings of the 58th Annual Meeting of the Association for Computational Linguistics, ACL 2020, Online, July 5-10, 2020*, pages 7881–7892. Association for Computational Linguistics.

Lei Sha. 2020. Gradient-guided unsupervised lexically constrained text generation. In *Proceedings of the 2020 Conference on Empirical Methods in Natural Language Processing (EMNLP)*, pages 8692–8703, Online. Association for Computational Linguistics.

Joel Shor, Dotan Emanuel, Oran Lang, Omry Tuval, Michael Brenner, Julie Cattiau, Fernando Vieira, Maeve McNally, Taylor Charbonneau, Melissa Nollstadt, and et al. 2019. Personalizing asr for dysarthric and accented speech with limited data. *Interspeech 2019*.

Eric Michael Smith, Diana Gonzalez-Rico, Emily Dinan, and Y-Lan Boureau. 2020. Controlling style in generated dialogue. *CoRR*, abs/2009.10855.

TherapyBox. 2021. Predictable: Text-to-speech aac app (accessed sept 2021).

Verbally. 2021. Verbally app (accessed sept 2021).

Keith Vertanen. 2013. A collection of conversational aac-like communications. In *The 15th International ACM SIGACCESS Conference on Computers and Accessibility, ASSETS '13, Bellevue, WA, USA, October 21-23, 2013*, pages 31:1–31:2. ACM.

Keith Vertanen and Per Ola Kristensson. 2011. The imagination of crowds: Conversational AAC language modeling using crowdsourcing and large data sources. In *Proceedings of the 2011 Conference on Empirical Methods in Natural Language Processing, EMNLP 2011, 27-31 July 2011, John McIntyre Conference Centre, Edinburgh, UK, A meeting of SIGDAT, a Special Interest Group of the ACL*, pages 700–711. ACL.

Ashwin Vijayakumar, Michael Cogswell, Ramprasaath Selvaraju, Qing Sun, Stefan Lee, David Crandall, and Dhruv Batra. 2018. Diverse beam search for improved description of complex scenes. *Proceedings of the AAAI Conference on Artificial Intelligence*, 32(1).

Thomas Wolf, Victor Sanh, Julien Chaumond, and Clement Delangue. 2019. Transfertransfo: A transfer learning approach for neural network based conversational agents. *CoRR*, abs/1901.08149.

Jonathan Wolpaw, Richard Bedlack, Domenic Reda, Robert Ringer, Patricia Banks, Theresa Vaughan, Susan Heckman, Lynn Mccane, Charles Carmack, Stefan Winden, Dennis Mcfarland, Eric Sellers, Hairong Shi, Tamara Paine, Donald Higgins, Albert Lo, Huned Patwa, Katherine Hill, Grant Huang, and Robert Ruff. 2018. Independent home use of a brain-computer interface by people with amyotrophic lateral sclerosis. *Neurology*, 91:10.1212/WNL.0000000000005812.

Heng-Da Xu, Xian-Ling Mao, Zewen Chi, Jing-Jing Zhu, Fanshu Sun, and Heyan Huang. 2020a. Generating informative dialogue responses with keywords-guided networks.

Peng Xu, Mostofa Patwary, Mohammad Shoeybi, Raul Puri, Pascale Fung, Anima Anandkumar, and Bryan Catanzaro. 2020b. MEGATRON-CNTRL: controllable story generation with external knowledge using large-scale language models. In *Proceedings of the 2020 Conference on Empirical Methods in Natural Language Processing, EMNLP 2020, Online, November 16-20, 2020*, pages 2831–2845. Association for Computational Linguistics.

Tianyi Zhang, Varsha Kishore, Felix Wu, Kilian Q. Weinberger, and Yoav Artzi. 2020a. Bertscore: Evaluating text generation with BERT. In *8th International Conference on Learning Representations, ICLR 2020, Addis Ababa, Ethiopia, April 26-30, 2020*. OpenReview.net.

Yizhe Zhang, Siqi Sun, Michel Galley, Yen-Chun Chen, Chris Brockett, Xiang Gao, Jianfeng Gao, Jingjing Liu, and Bill Dolan. 2020b. DIALOGPT : Large-scale generative pre-training for conversational response generation. In *Proceedings of the 58th Annual Meeting of the Association for Computational Linguistics: System Demonstrations*, pages 270–278, Online. Association for Computational Linguistics.

Yizhe Zhang, Siqi Sun, Michel Galley, Yen-Chun Chen, Chris Brockett, Xiang Gao, Jianfeng Gao, Jingjing

Liu, and Bill Dolan. 2020c. Dialogpt: Large-scale generative pre-training for conversational response generation. In *ACL, system demonstration*.

Appendix

A Human Evaluation Setup Details

Human evaluation of our system is split into three tasks: task 1 for collecting keywords and corresponding responses from humans. Task 2 involved the crowd workers on Amazon Mechanical Turk interact with our system. We used the keyword suggestions from our extractive and generative keyword predictor models and also the human-generated keywords. We run our controlled response generation pipeline on these keywords to obtain relevant responses. In this task, we first present the turkers with the conversation context as shown in 5. We also present 9 keyword suggestions - 3 from the extractive keyword predictor, 3 from the generative keyword predictor and 3 keywords generated by humans (from task 1). Figure 6 shows this step. Choosing one of these keywords, brings up responses from the human responses generated from Task1, and our controllable response generation model. We use kw_loss model with γ=0.005 and diverse beam search to generate the responses. The users can choose one of the responses and further edit, or enter his/her own response in the box provided.

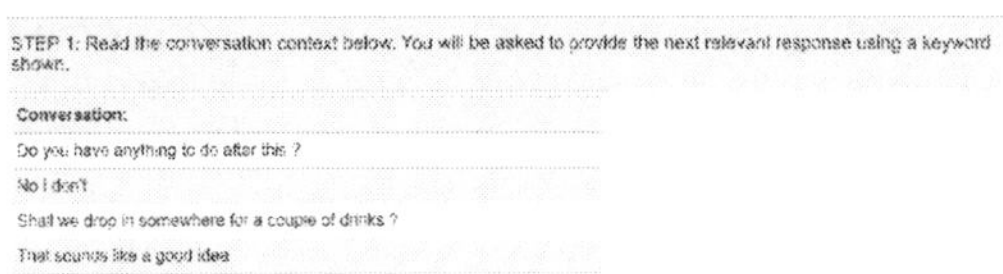

Figure 5: Shows the step 1 for Task 2 on the MTurk study. Here the turkers are presented with the conversation context.

We then present a questionnaire to the turkers - asking them to answer on a likert scale, some questions about why they chose a particular keyword/responses. At the end, turkers are shown a virtual keyboard as you can see in Figure 7 and asked to type in the response that they chose/edited. Using their physical keyboard is disabled for this part of the task - this is to ensure that the turkers use the virtual keyboard and generate the given text. This data enables us to compare the time it took to complete a single interaction and the time it takes to actually type in the entire response (future work).

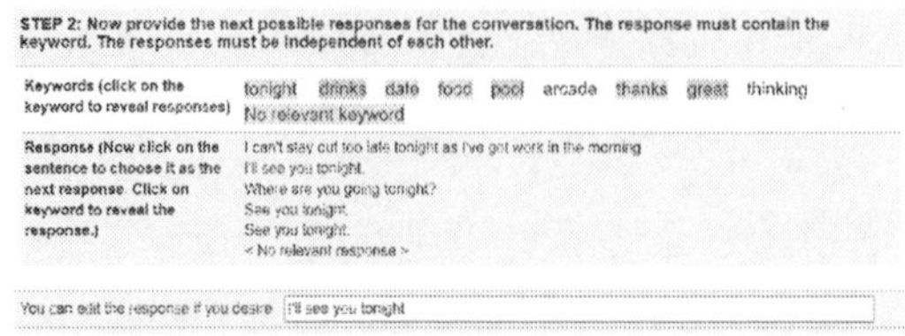

Figure 6: Shows the step 2 for Task 2 on the MTurk study. Here the turkers are shown 9 keywords (generated from keyword predictor models and humans from task 1). Choosing one of them allows them to see the response generated from our models, and human-generated ground truth response, that can be chosen.

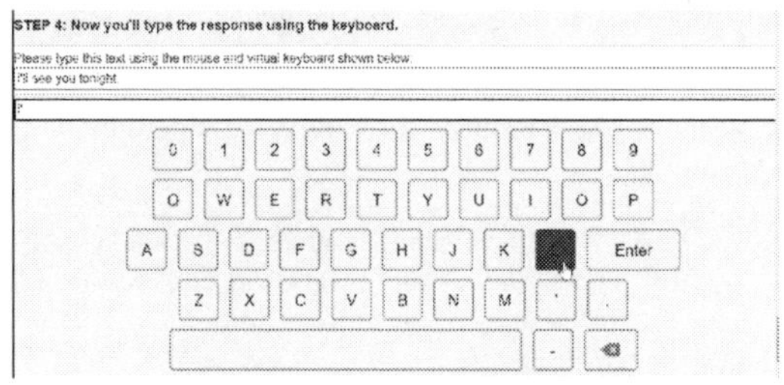

Figure 7: Shows the step 4 for Task 2 on the MTurk study. Step 3 is questionnaire with radio button options which is not shown above.

B Experiments

We present the effect of varying the γ coefficient in the keyword-based loss models. These results are presented in table 3. Please note that when $\gamma = 0$, the model is the $kw\_context$ model. We see from the table that increasing γ increases the KIA, which matches our intuition, and reaches close to 75% when $\gamma = 1$. However, we see that this is optimal when $\gamma = 0.005$. Similarity metrics such as BLEURT see a drop as we increase γ with the lowest at 1. Also, Response Quality deteriorate heavily with context coherence, diversity and fluency metrics. While the higher γ tries to increasingly encourage the model to generate the keyword in the sentence, this is at the cost of the overall quality of the response. Hence, in all of the experiments and results reported in the paper, we fix $\gamma = 0.005$, unless otherwise specified.

C Sample Model Outputs

In Table 4, we present the outputs from the various models - for a given context and keyword. We show the sample outputs from the no_kw, $kw\_context$, $kwloss\_0.005$, $kwloss\_sim\_loss\_glove$ models and the ground truth. We see that the keywords-based models are able to effectively induce the

	KWI Accuracy	Similarity	BLEURT	Context	Diversity	Fluency	PPL
coeff=0	0.672	0.539	**-0.607**	0.568	**1.789**	0.403	**41.752**
coeff=0.005	0.694	**0.542**	-0.609	0.579	1.726	**0.407**	43.115
coeff=0.01	0.681	0.538	-0.629	**0.581**	1.641	0.406	45.749
coeff=0.1	0.690	0.508	-0.846	0.519	0.888	0.397	92.567
coeff=1	**0.746**	0.527	-0.826	0.468	0.695	0.373	90.070

Table 3: Examining the effect of γ

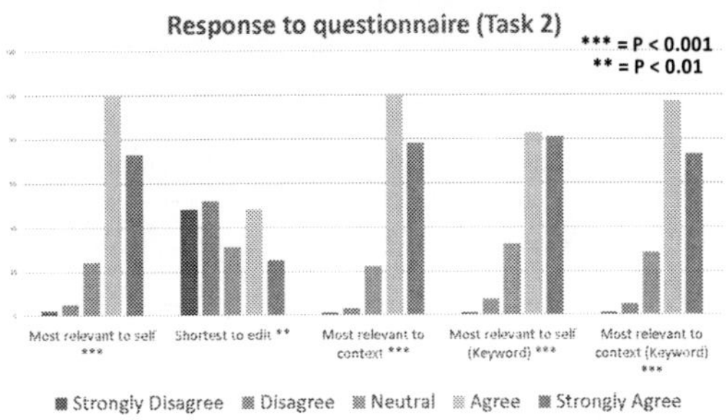

Figure 8: Shows the responses to the questionnaire in Task 2. (One-Sample Wilcoxon Signed Rank Test (mu=0)).

keywords into the generated sentence.

D Keyword Control with Multiple Inputs

Table 5 shows the results from our experiments with training the modesl with multiple keywords as control. We see that $kw\_sim\_loss\_wordnet - 1$ performs well on several metrics. We plan to look into these models further as part of future work.

E Human Evaluation Additional Results

Figure 8 shows some statistics on the responses to the questions asked to the user after the above interaction. The plot shows that most people agree/strongly agree that they picked the keyword/response because it seemed relevant to the context or it resonated with the response in their mind. The plot also shows that people did not choose a response because it was short to edit. This analysis shows that our procedure of suggesting keywords followed by relevant responses is the right strategy for building the controllable response generation system.

F User Study

F.1 User Interface

Figure 9 shows the user interface for our system. The top area shows the placeholder for the interlocutor's voice input which is converted to text for the model using ASR. The interface is divided into two parts, the top area is further split into two panes 1) the left pane brings up the keywords generated from the keyword predictor. Custom keywords can be added using the 'Add Custom Keyword' button. Once a keyword choice is made, 2) the right pane displays the generated responses from the keyword-based response generation model. The bottom area shows the virtual keyboard with buttons large enough to enable the gaze-tracker to detect gaze without ambiguities. Picking one of the generated responses from the right phrase pane, populates it into the textarea which can be edited by the user if needed. The 'Speak' button converts the user's response to speech. Finally, the chat window on the bottom-right keeps track of the ongoing conversation for the user's reference.

F.2 Conversational Goals/Tasks

The users were presented with 4 tasks out of which they could choose any two(without communicating the information with the interlocutor), to carry out a conversation as natural as possible. The 4 tasks revolved around the assistive usecase and as below:

- Invite an interlocutor to a party hosted by the user or to watch a movie (details: when, where and what time).
- Request the interlocutor to get some groceries (details: what and from where)
- Convey to the interlocutor that the user has a bad headache and needs help in setting up a doctors appointment (details: when)
- Convey to the interlocutor that the user is hungry and wants something for lunch. (details: what)

A conversation is considered to be complete or successful when the user is able to convey the goal of the interaction to the interlocutor along with the details associated with the goal. Each session with

Context	**Speaker1**: John , I'd like you to meet Charles Brown , our new manager at the airport . **Speaker2**: Yes , certainly . How can I recognize him ? **Speaker1**: He is short , well-built , and he's got light blond hair . **Speaker2**: Is there anything else ?	**Speaker1**: Please tell me something about your insurance background . **Speaker2**: I majored in international banking at college so I took many insurance courses . And I worked at an insurance company for my graduation field work . **Speaker1**: Why do you want to be an insurance agent ? . **Speaker2**:I care about people and I know the importance of insurance . **Speaker1**: Do you have any work experience in promotion ?
Keyword	***mustache***	***salesman***
NoKeyword	*Yes, he is tall, but he is slim.*	*Yes, I have been promoted twice. I have been promoted twice as well.*
kwcontext	*No, he has a very nice mustache.*	*Yes, I have worked as a salesman for a few years.*
KwLoss_0.005	*He has a rather bushy facial beard and a moustache.*	*Yes. I have a sales job as a salesman in a car dealership.*
kwloss_sim_glove	*No, that's it. He has a rather light mustache, too.*	*Yes, I have been a salesman for two years.*
GroundTruth	*He has a mustache , if I remember correctly , and a light complexion .*	*Yes , I do . I have worked as a salesman for P and G Company Ltd .*

Context	**Speaker1**: Were you in a leadership position when you were a college student ? **Speaker2**: Yes . I was president of the Student Council of our university . **Speaker1**: Did you get any honors or awards at your university ? **Speaker2**: Yes . I was elected Excellent Party Member for four academic years . **Speaker1**: Were you involved in any club activities at your university ? **Speaker2**: Yes . I was a member of the Student Poetry Society . I like writing poems in my spare time	**Speaker1**: Do you have a free moment ? **Speaker2**: Sure . What do you need ? **Speaker1**: I'm having some trouble . How do you use this printer ? . **Speaker2**: Well , first you have to turn this switch on . **Speaker1**: Silly me
Keyword	***extracurricular***	***button***
NoKeyword	*What kinds of poems did you write?*	*It's not complicated.*
kwcontext	*Did you have any extracurricular activities?*	*Then push the button.*
KwLoss_0.005	*Were you involved in any extracurricular activities?*	*Now press this button.*
kwloss_sim_glove	*What was your extracurricular activities?*	*Then press the button.*
GroundTruth	*What extracurricular activities did you usually take part in at your college ?*	*Now press this button .*

Table 4: Sample conversation contexts and comparison of different model outputs

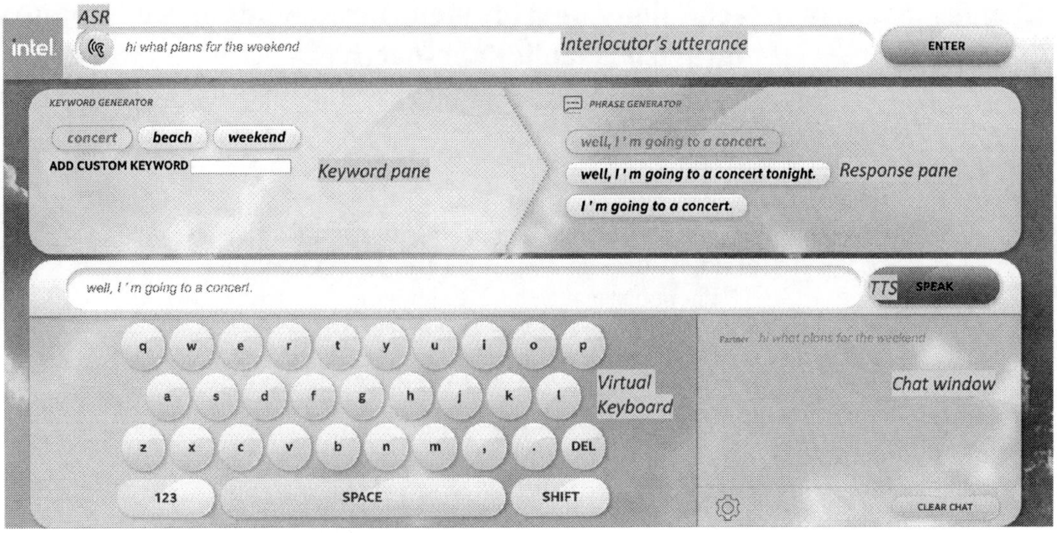

Figure 9: Cue-bot interface

Multiple Keywords	KIA	Similarity	BLEURT	BERT Score	Context	Diversity	Fluency	PPL↓
no_kw	0.041	0.271	-1.035	0.868/0.836/0.851	0.541	1.592	0.407	**39.098**
kw_context	0.293	0.607	**-0.499**	**0.895/0.857/0.875**	0.489	**1.396**	0.399	75.300
kw_loss	0.300	0.604	-0.524	0.894/0.856/0.874	**0.492**	1.354	0.412	83.971
kw_sim_loss_glove-1	**0.302**	**0.610**	-0.535	**0.895/0.857/0.875**	0.487	1.366	0.416	84.367
kw_sim_loss_wordnet-1	0.287	0.600	-0.525	0.894/0.856/0.874	0.488	1.351	**0.417**	80.403
kw_sim_loss_glove	0.293	0.598	-0.511	0.893/0.855/0.873	0.479	1.344	0.412	80.258
kw_sim_loss_wordnet	0.300	0.607	-0.518	0.894/0.856/0.875	0.483	1.364	0.416	79.888

Table 5: Performance of the various controllable models for multiple keyword input (γ = 0.005). Label "-1" indicates that we set $sim(k, kw) = 1$ in equation 3.

a user lasted between 60 minutes to 90 minutes. The first 30 minutes were spent in explaining the study to the user and helping the user familiarize with the gaze-tracker and the Opti-key mouse functions. Post user-study, a survey was sent to the users to get feedback about the experience with the system.

Challenges in assistive technology development for an endangered language: an Irish (Gaelic) perspective

Ailbhe Ni Chasaide, Emily Barnes, Neasa Ní Chiaráin, Rónán McGuirk, Oisín Morrin, Muireann Nic Corcráin, Julia Cummins
Phonetics and Speech Laboratory
Trinity College Dublin
anichsid@tcd.ie

Abstract

This paper describes three areas of assistive technology development which deploy the resources and speech technology for Irish (Gaelic), newly emerging from the ABAIR initiative. These include (i) a screenreading facility for visually impaired people, (ii) an application to help develop phonological awareness and early literacy for dyslexic people (iii) a speech-enabled AAC system for non-speaking people. Each of these is at a different stage of development and poses unique challenges: these are discussed along with the approaches adopted to address them. Three guiding principles underlie development. Firstly, the sociolinguistic context and the needs of the community are essential considerations in setting priorities. Secondly, development needs to be language sensitive. The need for skilled researchers with a deep knowledge of Irish structure is illustrated in the case of (ii) and (iii), where aspects of Irish linguistic structure (phonological, morphological and grammatical) and the striking differences from English pose challenges for systems aimed at bilingual Irish-English users. Thirdly, and most importantly, the users and their support networks are central – not as passive recipients of ready-made technologies, but as active partners at every stage of development, from design to implementation, evaluation and dissemination.

1 Introduction

This paper discusses ongoing research which aims to ensure that the emerging speech technologies and resources emerging for Irish (Gaelic) are made available in assistive technologies that cater for those with disabilities.

The rapid advances and increasingly ubiquitous use of speech and language technologies is viewed as a 'digital timebomb' within endangered language communities (Evans, 2018). Like other endangered languages, Irish lives in the shadow of a 'major' world language (English). In such a bilingual context, the unequal provision of speech and language technologies in the two languages is obliging native speakers to switch to the major language in more and more domains of activity – accelerating the already catastrophic rate at which endangered languages are being lost.

Nonetheless, these same technologies can offer a lifeline that might defuse this timebomb (Ní Chasaide et al., 2019a). Making the language part of this digital revolution provides the community with new ways to document, maintain and revive their language (Ní Chasaide et al., 2019a).

The ABAIR initiative has for a number of years been developing speech (linguistic) resources and core speech technologies for Irish. Text-to-speech synthesis (TTS) systems have been developed and are publicly available[1]. A beta automatic speech recognition system (ASR) is now also developed and will be launched later this year. Developing core technologies without parallel development of assistive technologies leaves people with

[1] www.abair.ie

Ninth Workshop on Speech and Language Processing for Assistive Technologies (SLPAT-2022), pages 80 - 87

disabilities without a voice – an invisible minority within a minority.

A central concern of ABAIR is to develop applications that make both resources and technologies readily available to all members of the language community. Unlike the situation of the 'major' world languages, where application development is driven by commercial concerns, for minority or endangered languages, the most urgent needs of the community should dictate development priorities. ABAIR is therefore developing applications targeting the general public, the educational sector and, importantly, those with speech and communication disabilities. The involvement of the community and of specific end-user groups is central in all this development.

This paper describes three areas of assistive technology, in which work is at different stages of development. These include (i) applications for visually impaired people, (ii) applications for dyslexic people, and (iii) applications for nonspeaking people. Sections 4, 5, and 6 outline the development so far in these areas. As essential background, Section 2 explains the socio-linguistic context, while Section 3 focusses on difficulties specific to minority and endangered languages.

While some aspects of our work are specific to the Irish context, many of the challenges – and the approaches to overcoming them – are relevant to the wider endangered language community, and especially to minority language users with disabilities who are doubly excluded from their language through want of appropriate assistive technologies.

2 The socio-linguistic context

Irish (Gaelic) is classified by UNESCO as definitely endangered (Moseley, 2012). It is spoken as a community language in Gaeltacht regions, mostly on the western seaboard (see Figure 1). Although there are over 96,000 people living in Gaeltacht areas, the language is losing ground. Irish is recognised as the first official language of Ireland and since 2007 as an official language of the EU.

In this paper we focus particularly on the needs of school-going children and adolescents. As the first official language of Ireland, Irish is a core subject for all in primary and secondary school. Furthermore, interest in Irish immersion education (where all the schooling is carried out through Irish) is burgeoning and has seen steady growth in recent years (Gaeloideachas, 2022). Thus, between Gaeltacht schools and Irish immersion schools outside the Gaeltacht, Irish is the language of education for more than 66,000 children in Ireland (Gaeloideachas, 2022). In these schools, almost one in ten students have additional educational needs (Nic Aindriú, Ó Duibhir & Travers, 2020).

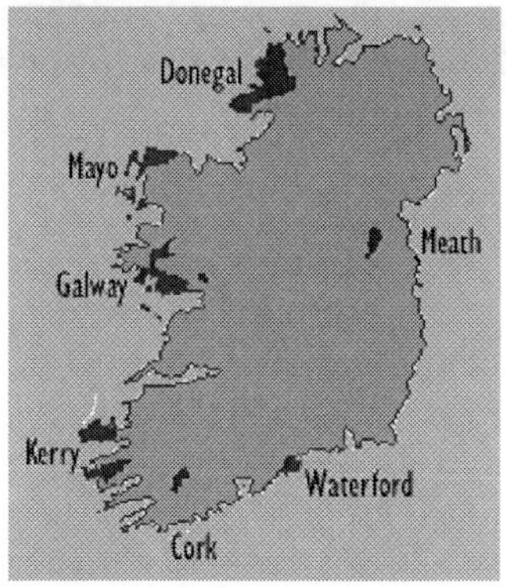

Figure 1: Map showing Gaeltacht (Irish speaking regions) in Ireland (shaded black).

The need for assistive technologies varies thus for different cohorts: in Gaeltacht native-speaker communities they can be key to inclusion in the family and in the life of the language community as well as being essential to participation in education. For those attending Irish immersion education outside the Gaeltacht, assistive technologies are paramount for engagement with the curriculum and for general communication with peers and teachers. For those in English-medium education, assistive technologies are essential to participate in Irish language learning and in the rich cultural online world of Irish.

Despite the transformative role of assistive technology in inclusion and education (e.g. Borg et al, 2021), despite the Government's commitment to promote the Irish language and despite the commitment to provide equal access to those with disabilities, the needs of the latter are largely overlooked when it comes to assistive technologies for Irish. There is little reference to access and disability in the above mentioned 20 Year Strategy for the Irish Language 2010-2030, and there is no reference to the Irish language or to bilingualism in the foremost report on the provision of assistive technology in Ireland (Cullen et al, 2010). This blind spot is also highlighted by the fact that speech and language therapists and other professionals are typically not trained to support bilingual people (Ní Chinnéide, 2009). The sense of disempowerment of those who need assistive technologies also emerges in a recent survey (Nic Corcráin, 2021)

3 Challenges for minority languages

To develop speech and language technologies (and applications) for a minority language brings many challenges, which are not necessarily appreciated by those involved in technology development in a 'major' language. As in many endangered languages, Irish has no spoken standard variety. There are 3 main dialects and a number of sub-dialects – all of which are deemed standard. The difference between dialects is considerable, particularly as pertains to pronunciation (prosodic and segmental) aspects and to the morphology. A written standard was established in 1958 with the publication of *An Caighdeán Oifigiúil* 'The Official Standard'. It is a compromised hybrid standard which draws on features from the individual dialects to suggest standardised spelling and grammar forms to be taught in schools. However, it is somewhat problematic, as the 'standard' does not correspond to the spoken forms of any given dialect.

These facts have many implications for speech technology development, and determine the parameters for technology development, if one aspires to technologies that are truly useful to the language communities. At the very least they need to cater for the various dialects of the potential users. Thus, in developing TTS for Irish in the ABAIR initiative, it was clear from the outset that multidialect speech synthesis (TTS) systems were a fundamental necessity. The current systems available on the ABAIR webpage include voices (male, female) in the three main dialects. Further dialects are being developed and ultimately all dialects targeted. Similarly, in developing speech recognition (ASR), it is crucial to be able to handle the different native speaker dialects. Consequently, corpus collection to date has focussed on native speakers from the different Gaeltacht areas. Not surprisingly therefore, the current beta ASR system is much more accurate for native speaker speech than for non-native-speaker speech, whether from proficient speaker or learner. Ultimately, the system will need to be capable of catering for all potential users.

The bilingual context of most endangered languages brings additional challenges. Code switching is frequent, and speech technologies need to be able to deal with it. For certain kinds of assistive technologies, linguistic differences between the endangered and 'major' language raises issues require language-specific resource development to underpin the technology.

4 An Irish screenreading facility

A screenreading facility for Irish has been developed as a plugin for the NVDA screenreader, prompted by urgent pleas from parents and grandparents of visually impaired children in the Gaeltacht or attending Irish-medium schools. For these children, the lack of access to written forms of Irish undermined their education (there are only 3 books available in Braille for Irish). Note that almost 55,000 people are blind or visually impaired in Ireland – 4,701 of whom are of school age (Central Statistics Office, 2016b)

With funding from the National Council for the Blind in Ireland (NCBI) a blind researcher worked with the ABAIR team to develop the NVDA screenreader plugin. It additionally provides simultaneous Braille output from the opensource Liblouis Braille translator[2] which has features that support screenreading programmes such as the NVDA system. The user chooses the 'speaker' (male or female) and controls for the speed of the spoken output. Note that very high speeds are often used for browsing by proficient readers, whereas young learners might need quite slow reading speeds. For those with some partial vision, text is highlighted and magnified as it is read out. Beyond the educational context, the screenreader allows the user to fully participate in the digital world, communicate with the lively online language community, keep up with current affairsas well as read, write and edit documents. The system was extensively tested with visually-impaired school children and a full technical description is available in McGuirk (2005).

5 Technology for those with dyslexia

The provision of a screenreader was primarily a matter of building an interface that would allow access to the ABAIR voices and facilities. In other areas, assistive technologies require in-depth

[2] www.liblouis.org

knowledge of the language structure and, in a given bilingual context, a knowledge of how the structure of the minority and major language differ. This linguistic knowledge supports the development of more effective solutions to challenges that may arise. Such is the case in the provision of applications for those with dyslexia, the most frequently reported additional educational need in Irish immersion schools (Nic Aindriú, Ó Duibhir & Travers, 2020). Assistance with Irish literacy teaching and training for pupils with dyslexia is frequently requested by teachers in Gaeltacht and Irish-medium schools. Tackling this issue involves much more than a technology interface - it requires much basic research to identify issues and build the additional linguistic resources needed to address them.

Phonemic awareness (an explicit awareness of the sound structure of the language; Goswami & Bryant, 1991), and an understanding of phonic rules (how sounds map to letters) have a key role in literacy acquisition, and often form a key part of dyslexia assessments and interventions.

Irish and English are very different in both (i) the phonemic sound systems and (ii) orthographic systems. This means that children need to learn two separate systems, one for each language. The most distinctive feature of Irish phonology is the set of velarised-palatalised consonant contrasts.

	Initial palatalised consonant	Orthographic transcription	Initial velarised consonant	Orthographic transcription
Front vowel	bʲi:	bí	bˠi:	buí
Back vowel	bʲo:	beo	bˠo:	bó

Figure 2: Phonological and Orthographic representations of an initial pair of velarised-palatalised consonants followed by (phonologically) front and back vowels.

This sound contrast is represented opaquely in the orthography, as the Latin alphabet does not allow for an effective doubling of consonantal letters. Thus, for a minimal pair like [lʲo:nˠ] *leon* 'lion' and [lˠo:nˠ] *lón* 'lunch' the same initial letter "l" is used to for the contrasting palatalised and velarised initial consonants. The quality difference is signalled by the nearest vowel letter. An adjacent "i" and "e" (front vowels) signal a palatalised consonant, while an adjacent "u", "o" and "ɑ" (back vowels) point to a velarised consonant. (See Figure 2). To sum up, the consonantal contrast is not overtly marked, and vowel letters can have different functions: they may represent an actual phoneme, or they may serve to denote the quality of an adjacent consonant (see Ní Chasaide, 1999).

This opaque representation of the sounds can be challenging for readers but is particularly challenging for those with dyslexia. Learners are largely not consciously aware of the consonantal contrast. Children outside of Gaeltacht areas often have little exposure to native speaker speech and may not acquire the sound contrasts which are important for understanding the writing system. The fact that all pupils are taught the phonics of English further impacts on their grasp of the sound and phonic systems of Irish.

Figure 3: Homepage of the Lón don Leon platform.

There is a dearth of resources for children with dyslexia in Irish. As the first step in tackling this question an interactive platform has been developed to train phonological awareness and early phonics skills. This platform, *Lón don Leon* 'Lunch for the Lion' is set on an imaginary Aran Island (see homepage in Figure 3), populated by characters and objects (like the lion and his lunch) which provide minimal pairs that illustrate the contrast. Specially written stories with graphics, musical ditties and quizzes aim to consolidate phonological awareness and memorisation of contrasts. When the phonological contrasts are acquired, further games make explicit how these sounds map to the orthographic letters.

The platform uses a mixture of prerecorded (songs and stories) and the ABAIR synthetic voices (in spelling activities). It is being presented as a learning platform for all – but is particularly critical for those with dyslexia. Having the synthetic voices is particularly helpful, as it brings the native speaker right into the classroom. The platform draws on previous linguistic and educational research (Ní Chasaide 1979, 1999; Barnes, 2017, 2021), and the hope is to launch it later this year.

In its current form, *Lón don Leon* is focussed on training and intervention. However, we envisage in the future that it will be extended to incorporate assessment materials that will address the dearth of screening and diagnostic assessments for dyslexia (Barnes 2017; Nic Aindriú, Ó Duibhir & Travers, 2021). Additional support materials for pupils with dyslexia and their teachers are also envisaged.

The development of *Lón don Leon* and its underpinning research has benefitted from extensive interaction with stakeholders (interviews with educational psychologists, discussions with educational professionals, testing with children and consultation with Irish language organisations).

6 Speech enabled AAC

A speech-generating AAC system allows the non-speaking user to select a series of images/words which are subsequently spoken aloud by the computer. Though many such systems exist for the English language, there is currently no such system available for Irish. As shown in a recent survey (Nic Corcráin, 2021) many people could benefit from such a system, including autistic people, as well as people with Cerebral Palsy, Parkinson's Disease, Alzheimer's disease and those with learning disabilities (Enderby et al, 2013).

There are many autistic children who attend and benefit from Irish immersion schools (Nic Aindriú, Ó Duibhir & Travers, 2020). The lack of a speech-generating AAC system in Irish means that non-speaking autistic children and children with communication disabilities are excluded de facto from fully participating in their language community, whether in the Gaeltacht or in Irish immersion schooling. There is an urgent need to develop such a system to remove the barriers preventing children from fully participating in school and in their communities, as well as from accessing their rich linguistic and cultural heritage. An Irish prototype AAC system has been developed within the open-source Coughdrop system. The bilingual context of users, and the linguistic structural features of Irish have a considerable impact on how AAC can be developed, as beyond the phonological and orthographic differences between Irish and English mentioned above, there are major differences in morphology, syntax and semantics. Irish is an inflected language: nouns and adjectives have a number of cases; there are numerous inflections of verbal forms; many classes of content words undergo initial mutations (alternation of the initial consonant in specific grammatical contexts – a feature of all Celtic languages). This means that content words have a large number of forms (written and spoken) when compared to English. For example, the word 'house' has just two forms in English (house, houses); in Irish it has many more (*teach, tí, tithe, theach, dteach, thithe, dtithe*). In the case of numerals there are different forms: for example, the word for 'two' may emerge as *dó, dhá, beirt, dhó* depending on the subject (human/non-human) and the grammatical context.

Differences also exist in the semantic domains of superficially cognate words such as 'know'. In English, there is a single term for knowing a person, a fact, a subject, a language, and a place. In Irish there are different terms depending on the object of the sentence (e.g., *aithne, ar eolas, fios/a fhios*). This makes it challenging to graft an Irish system into an existing English- schema.

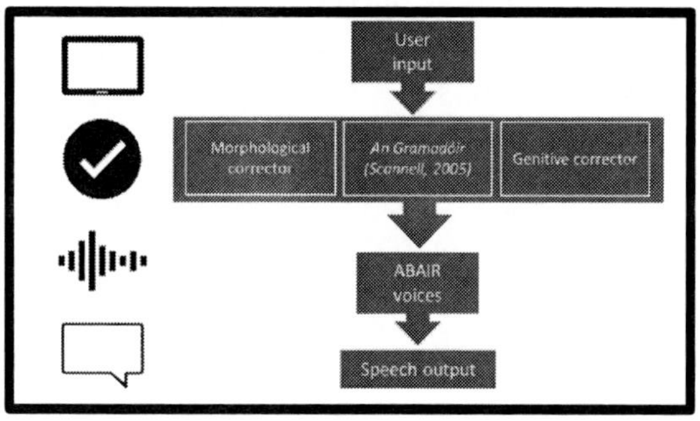

Figure 4: A schematic representation of the Irish AAC system currently under development

As a way of going from a sequence of images to a sentence with a correct grammatical form, the system currently under development uses three grammar checkers and correctors: (1) a morphological corrector based on hand-coded grammatical rules provides corrections for certain inflected forms; then the input is processed by (2) an open-source grammar checking engine *An Gramadóir,* built using language-independent software for under-resourced languages (Scannell, 2005), and finally (3) a genitive checker corrects nouns in the genitive case. As illustrated in Figure 4, the user inputs a string of symbols with their associated root lexical forms into the Coughdrop system. The lexical string is then sent to the AAC API, which allows for grammatical correction by the three correctors described above. The corrected version is then sent to the ABAIR TTS API, and the sound files generated are returned to the Coughdrop system as spoken output. Again, the user chooses the dialect, the speaker and the speed.

The bilingual context in which the system will be used provides further challenges that have a bearing on the system design. Speech output from AAC devices involves using motor sequences to select items. Therefore, it is aided by visuo-spatial representations rather than phonological (sound-based) ones (Dukhovny & Gahl, 2014). When using such devices, people remember and access words through motor plans, as they do when typing (Dukhovny & Gahl, 2014). More research and on-the-ground testing will be needed to establish whether one should aim to optimise the layout of symbols in order to optimise the motor plans in both Irish and English. In practice, this would mean maintaining consistency in the positions of the buttons in each language version of the AAC system. These are still open questions that require research and ongoing evaluation with users.

As with the other developments discussed here, the strong initial impetus for this project came from the community. Speech therapists working with non-speaking clients have been requesting Irish AAC, and a kickstart was provided in an urgent request by a parent whose children require such a system and who wanted to work with us to develop one. Her children need Irish AAC in order to fully access the curriculum in their Irish-medium school, as well as to communicate with their Gaeltacht-based family members and friends. More recently this parent has joined the research team.

7 Conclusions

Developing assistive technologies for an endangered/minority language involves a great deal more than interfacing and simple translation. An understanding of the language structure is critical to many of the technologies, and the bilingual context in which the users use the technologies can have important implications on how we design them. For example, the AAC system might require differences in design depending on whether the users of Irish are L1 or L2. In the case of devices for developing phonological awareness and early literacy training, the L1-L2 differences are the key basis for the system design. Other linguistic factors such as the great diversity of dialects, and the lack of a single spoken standard, is something that is likely to occur in many endangered languages.

One advantage of the current developments for Irish is that the core technologies are being developed in parallel with the applications described here. This means that the priorities in the core developments are guided by an understanding of the needs of the potential end users. While the dialect diversity is currently catered for with our Irish synthetic voices, the provision for children's voices (for the various dialects) is being targeted for future research given how necessary it is for many of the users, both in the disability and educational spheres. These same considerations are central to the current and future development of automatic speech recognition for Irish. Our current prototype has been optimised for native speaker adults of the different dialects and extending this to children's speech will be the important next step. From the above it is clear that a multidisciplinary team is ideally required involving researchers who not only have the prerequisite technical skills but also a deep understanding of the structure of Irish, allied to an understanding of the bilingual and social context. Finding skilled interdisciplinary researchers has proven to date to be the greatest challenge to ABAIR's progress.

In developing assistive technologies, it is important to work with existing open-source systems where such are available. As a guiding principal, ABAIR aims to ensure that the outputs are cost-free and made readily available on the ABAIR website.

The language community and the network of end users for particular disability applications have been central to the developments discussed here. Ultimately, the user and the user's support networks (teachers, family, carers, therapists) have had a role – not as passive recipients of ready-made prototypes but rather as active partners from the outset with input into every stage of development from design to implementation, evaluation and dissemination.

Acknowledgments

We gratefully acknowledge An Roinn Ealaíon, Oidhreachta agus Gaeltachta which support the ABAIR Project, as part of An *Stráitéis 20 bliain don Ghaeilge, 2010-2030*. We also gratefully acknowledge the support of An Chomhairle um Oideachas Gaeltachta agus Gaelscolaíochta

(COGG), as well as the National Council for the Blind of Ireland for their support.

References

Barnes, (2017). 'Dyslexia Assessment and Reading Interventions for Pupils in Irish-Medium Education: Insights into current practice and considerations forimprovement'. Unpublished M.Phil thesis, Trinity College Dublin.

Barnes, E. (2017) Dyslexia Assessment and Reading Interventions for Pupils in Irish- Medium Education: Insights into current practice and considerations for improvement, M.Phil. Dissertation, School of Linguistic, Speech and Communication Sciences, Trinity College Dublin, Ireland

Barnes. (2021). Predicting dual-language literacy attainment in Irish-English bilinguals: language-specific and language-universal contributions. PhD thesis, Trinity College Dublin.

Borg, J., Zhang, W., Smith, E. M., & Holloway, C. (2021). Introduction to the companion papers to the global report on assistive technology. *Assistive technology*, *33*(sup1), 1-2.

Central Statistics Office. 2016. Profile 10 Education, Skills and the Irish Language. Dublin: Stationery Office. Available at http: https://www.cso.ie/en/releasesandpublications/ep/p-cp10esil/p10esil/ilg/ (accessed February 2022)

Cullen, K., McAnaney, D., Dolphin, C., Delaney, S., & Stapleton, P. (2012). Research on the provision of Assistive Technology in Ireland and other countries to support independent living across the life cycle. Work Research Centre, Dublin.

Dukhovny, E., & Gahl, S. (2014). Manual motor-plan similarity affects lexical recall on a speech-generating device: Implications for AAC users. *Journal of communication disorders*, *48*, 52-60.

Enderby, P., Judge S., Creer, S., John, A. (2013) Examining the need for, and provison of, AAC in the United Kingdom. Research Report. Communication Matters

Evans, G. (2018). Report on Language Equality in the Digital Age. Retrieved online 22/11/2019 from: http://www.europarl.europa.eu/doceo/document/A-8- 2018-0228_EN.html

Gaeloideachas (2020). *Statistics.* Available at: https://gaeloideachas.ie/i-am-a-researcher/statistics/ (accessed February 2022)

Goswami, U., & Bryant, P. (1990). Phonological skills and learning to read. Hillsdale, NJ: Lawrence Erlbaum.

Government of Ireland (2010). 20-Year Strategy for the Irish Language 2010-2030. Available at: https://www.gov.ie/en/policy-information/2ea63-20-year-strategy-for-the-irish-language/

McGuirk, R. (2015). Exploration of the Use of Irish Language Synthesis with a Screen Reader in the Teaching of Irish to Pupils with Vision Impairment, M.Phil. Dissertation, School of Linguistic, Speech and Communication Sciences, Trinity College Dublin, Ireland.

Moseley, C. (2012). The UNESCO Atlas of the World's Languages in Danger: Context and Process. http://www.dspace.cam.ac.uk/handle/1810/243434

Ní Chasaide, A. (1979). Acoustic Study of Laterals in Donegal Irish and Hiberno-English. (Masters Thesis, University of Bangor).

Ní Chasaide, A. (1999). Irish. In Handbook of the International Phonetic Association, pp. 111– 116. Cambridge: Cambridge University Press.

Ní Chasaide, A., Ní Chiaráin, N., Berthelsen, H., Wendler, C., Murphy, A., Barnes, E., Gobl, C. (2019a). Can we Defuse the Digital Timebomb? Linguistics, Speech Technology and the Irish Language Community. Proceedings of the Language Technologies for All (LT4All), pp. 177–181. Paris, UNESCO Headquarters.

Ní Chasaide, A., Ní Chiaráin, N., Berthelsen, H., Wendler, C., Murphy, A., Barnes, E., Gobl, C. (2019b). Leveraging Phonetic and Speech Research for Language Revitalisation and Mainetnance, Proceedings of ICPhS, Melbourne.

Ní Chinnéide, Deirdre. 2009. The Special Educational Needs of Bilingual (Irish-English) Children, 52. POBAL, Education and Training. Available online: https://dera.ioe.ac.uk/11010/7/de1_09_83755__special_needs_of_bilingual_children_research_report_final_version_Redacted.pdf (accessed on 17 December 2016).

Nic Aindriú, S., Ó Duibhir, P., & Travers, J. (2020). The prevalence and types of special educational needs in Irish immersion primary schools in the Republic of Ireland. *European Journal of Special Needs Education*, *35*(5), 603-619.

Nic Corcráin, M. (2021). 'AAC don Ghaeilge': A needs analysis survey for the development of Irish language augmentative communication devices for people with speech difficulties. Unpublished M.Phil. thesis, Trinity College Dublin.

Stenson, N. and Hickey, T. M. (2014) In defense of decoding. Journal of Celtic Language Learning, 18, 11-40

Stephanidis, C., (Ed.) (2001). User Interfaces for All: Concepts, Methods and Tools. Lawrence Erlbaum Associates

Author Index

Association for Computational Linguistics
209 N. Eighth Street
Stroudsburg, Pennsylvania 18360

CURRAN ASSOCIATES INC.
proceedings.com

ISBN 978-1-7138-6751-7
9 781713 867517